The Mysterious Bible Codes

The Mysterious Bible Codes

by Grant R. Jeffrey

WORD PUBLISHING

NASHVILLE

A Thomas Nelson Company

Unless otherwise noted, Scripture quotations are from the KING JAMES VERSION of the Bible.

Scripture quotations marked NASB are from the NEW AMERICAN STANDARD BIBLE (R), Copyright © The Lockman Foundation 1960, 1962, 1968, 1971, 1972, 1973, 1975, 1977. Used by permission.

ISBN 0-8499-1325-X

Printed in the United States of America.

Contents

Introduction

1

Chapter 1
The Bible Codes Phenomenon

17

Chapter 2
The Ancient Discovery of the Bible Codes

33

Chapter 3
The Rediscovery of the Bible Codes in Modern Times

43

Chapter 4
Some Cautions about Bible Codes

57

Chapter 5
New Bible Code Discoveries
65

Chapter 6
The Yeshua Codes
89

Chapter 7
The Messiah Codes
103

Chapter 8
A Response to Critics of the Yeshua Codes
135

Chapter 9
A Response to Christian Critics of the Bible Codes
151

Chapter 10
The Discovery of Bible Codes in the Greek New Testament
169

Chapter 11
The Implications of the Bible Codes
181

Appendix
189

Notes
193

The Hebrew Alphabet

Sefardi Pronunciation

Numerical Value	Phonetics Form	Letters	Final Form
1	aleph	א	
2	bet, vet	ב	
3	gimmel	ג	
4	dalet	ד	
5	hey	ה	
6	vav	ו	
7	zayin	ז	
8	chet	ח	
9	tet	ט	
10	yod	י	
20	kaf	כ	ך
30	lamed	ל	
40	mem	מ	ם
50	nun	נ	ן
60	samek	ס	
70	ayin	ע	
80	pey, feh	פ	ף
90	tzadi	צ	ץ
100	qof	ק	
200	resh	ר	
300	shin, sin	ש	ש
400	tav	ת	

Note: Hebrew is written and read from right to left.

Although the Hebrew alphabet contains twenty-two individual letters, it also uses several final forms of some letters when they occur at the end of a word. These final-form letters represent the same letter as the regular form and do not change the meaning of the word. Bible Codes analysis treats the regular form and the final form of a letter identically. This variation of certain Hebrew letters is very similar to the English use of the lower case or upper case of a particular letter, such as *a* or *A*.

Introduction

The whole world is talking about the remarkable phenomenon known as the Bible Codes. It has been the subject of newspaper and magazine articles (including *TIME* and *Newsweek*), best-selling books, and radio and television shows. Is it possible that God has actually hidden a series of encoded words in the text of the Bible that reveals His supernatural knowledge of historical and current events? Is this phenomenon genuine? Are the claims about the Bible Codes true? If they are, the Bible Codes phenomenon provides powerful additional evidence that the Bible is truly the inspired Word of God.

When I first heard about the codes during a trip to Israel in the late 1980s, I was quite skeptical, but after more than ten years of careful evaluation of the evidence, I am convinced that the codes are genuine. The Bible Codes provide remarkable details about historical events that transpired thousands of years after the biblical text was written. Who but God Himself could have placed these codes in the Holy Scriptures?

In view of my own initial skepticism, I am not offended in the slightest when someone tells me that they cannot accept the authenticity of the Bible Codes. However, after almost ten years of research, I am more persuaded than ever that God has placed the Bible Codes within the text of the Bible to prove to this skeptical generation that He alone is the true author who inspired the written record of His revelation to humanity.

I trust that this in-depth study of *The Mysterious Bible Codes* will both fascinate and enlighten you as we explore the documented research that examines the phenomenon of the Bible Codes from a Christian perspective. You will learn how Bible students around the world are discovering new codes for themselves using sophisticated Bible search software programs. In addition to discussing all of the issues raised by this extraordinary discovery, I will attempt to provide comprehensive answers to the legitimate questions and objections to the Bible Codes, raised over the last few years by atheists, Christians, and Jews.

In light of the fact that the Bible has been studied extensively by hundreds of millions of Jews and Christians over the last thirty-five hundred years, some readers have asked how anyone in our generation could possibly discover something new about the Bible. This is a legitimate question. However, the surprising answer is that many new discoveries regarding the truths of the Holy Scriptures have actually been found in our generation.

For example, the discoveries made at archeological digs in the last one hundred and fifty years have given mankind new evidence of the absolute historical reliability of the ancient biblical text. Dr. Nelson Glueck, the greatest Jewish archeologist of this century, spent his life exploring the land of Israel in his search for archeological artifacts. As a result of his many discoveries, Dr. Glueck concluded that the Bible was totally accurate in every area where he compared the Bible text with the most recent archeological evidence.

Dr. Glueck summarized the results of the thousands of archeological discoveries made during the last century: "As a matter of fact, however, it may be stated categorically that no archeological discovery has ever controverted a biblical reference. Scores of archaeological findings have been made which confirm in clear outline or in exact detail historical statements in the Bible."[1]

Some of the most fascinating code research for Christians includes Yacov Rambsel's marvelous discovery of forty-one encoded words naming Jesus and His disciples, Mary, Joseph, and many other personalities in the life of Christ (including King Herod and the high priest Caiaphas). These names are encoded in a messianic prophecy, known as the Suffering Servant prophecy (Isaiah 52–53), that foretells details of the trial and crucifixion of Jesus Christ more than seven centuries before He was born.

In my opinion, the discovery of the Yeshua Codes revealing Jesus of Nazareth as the true Messiah provides the final "seal of approval."

It is not surprising to me that, from time to time, we would discover new types of evidence in the text of the Scriptures as well as in the world of science and archeology. An interesting quotation from the Christian writer Joseph Butler illustrates this point: "Nor is it at all incredible that a book which has been so long in the possession of mankind, should contain many truths as yet undiscovered."[2]

A Caution Regarding the Bible Codes

Like other types of Bible study, the Bible Codes are vulnerable to misuse. The following are some important cautions to keep in mind regarding the Bible Codes. These cautions are treated in depth in chapter 4.

> The Bible Codes cannot be used to foretell future events.
> The Bible Codes do not contain any hidden theological or doctrinal messages.
> The Bible Codes have nothing to do with numerology.

What Are the Bible Codes?

Throughout history, spies have used the technique of hiding encoded words in documents or letters to send secret messages. For example, an American spy working in a British fort during the Revolutionary War might have written an innocent-sounding letter to his mother in which he chatted about his health, the weather, et cetera. However, when his commander intercepted the letter, he would circle every twelfth letter to read the real, secret message: "400 soldiers and 22 cannons."

In a similar manner as the spy's code, the Bible Codes are meaningful words encoded in the Bible in a pattern that code researchers call "equidistant letter sequence" (ELS). The hidden word or phrase is discovered by skipping equal numbers of letters (e.g., every 7th letter). For example, researchers discovered that the word "Israel" ישראל is spelled out at equally spaced intervals of less than 100 letters only twice in the first 10,000 letters of Genesis. Within a short passage of only five verses in Genesis 1:30–2:3, the researchers found the word "Israel" ישראל by skipping every 7 letters and again by skipping every 50 letters. Interestingly, Jews around the world recite this passage in Genesis, known as the *Kiddush*, every seventh day on the Sabbath.

In Bible Code notation, the word *interval* indicates the number of Hebrew letters that are skipped in the original biblical passage to spell out the encoded word at equally spaced intervals (ELS). If the interval number in parentheses is positive (e.g., 22), the encoded word begins at the indicated passage and reads right to left, skipping the indicated number of Hebrew letters. However, if the interval number in parentheses is preceded by a minus sign (e.g., -13), the encoded word begins at the indicated passage and reads left to right, skipping the indicated number of Hebrew letters.

Although there is evidence that some Jewish rabbis knew of the existence of Bible Codes in the past, the development of high-speed computers provided the first opportunity to systematically search the Scriptures to discover how prevalent and extensive the phenomenon of Bible Codes actually is. Almost thirteen years ago a group of Israeli researchers including Dr. Eliyahu Rips developed a computer search program that can search the Hebrew text of the Bible. Initially, they found meaningfully encoded words that were thematically linked, such as "nail" and "hammer." These word pairs were located in closer proximity to each other than random chance would suggest possible.

As the researchers continued to study this phenomenon, they discovered that many of the ELS encoded words they found related to events and personalities from ancient times to this present generation. Moreover, these coded words were interlaced in intricate patterns in the text at evenly spaced intervals, reading both forward and backward. The scientists realized that these ELS encoded letters formed words and associations of such complexity and intricate design that it was impossible that the letter patterns could have occurred by random chance.

In particular, Dr. Rips discovered key words encoded repeatedly in a specific biblical passage about the same subject as the encoded words. The word "Eden," for example, is encoded sixteen times within the relatively short passage of Genesis 2:4–10, the account of God creating man and placing him in Eden. Statistical probability would expect to find only five accidental ELS occurrences of "Eden" in a passage of this length. The odds of sixteen "Eden's" occurring by random chance in such a short passage were calculated by Daniel Michaelson, Associate Professor of Mathematics at Hebrew University and the University of California (UCLA), as being 1 chance in 10,000.[3]

Dr. Michaelson also reported an interesting code pattern dealing with God's creation of vegetation in Genesis 2. Twenty-five different Hebrew names of trees are encoded within the text of this one chapter. The laws of probability indicate that the odds against this occurring by chance are 100,000 to 1.[4]

Thousands of detailed encoded patterns such as these have been discovered in the Hebrew text of the ancient Scriptures. After exhaustive statistical analysis, mathematics and computer experts conclude that these patterns of encoded words could not have occurred by chance, nor could an author purposely produce this phenomenon. Many of the researchers have concluded that only a divine intelligence could have directed Moses to record this precise text of Scripture thousands of years ago.

Codes about Hanukkah and the Hasmoneans

The wicked Syrian king Antiochus IV slaughtered tens of thousands of Jews who refused to worship him. Antiochus IV stopped the Temple sacrifice in 168 B.C. He then defiled the Altar by sacrificing a pig on it, provoking a Jewish rebellion led by an old man named Mattathias and his five sons. This resulted in a spectacular war of religious independence. The sons, led by Judas Maccabaeus ("the Hammer"), defeated the Syrian army against impossible odds in 165 B.C. The Jews reconquered the Temple site on the twenty-fourth day of the ninth month, exactly three years to the day after Antiochus IV had stopped the daily sacrifice.

The Jews cleansed the sacred Temple (1 Maccabees 4:52–54) and reinstituted Temple worship. The Jewish Talmud claims that a priest found a one-day supply of the sacred oil hidden in a wall of the Temple. When the oil was used to light the lamp, it miraculously lasted for the full eight days of the celebration. The Feast of Dedication is commemorated by the annual eight-day Hanukkah celebration. This festival, representing the inextinguishable nature of the Jewish faith in God, was celebrated also by Jesus Christ (John 10:22–23).

The Israeli researchers mentioned earlier found the encoded ELS word "Hanukkah," which refers to the festival (at a -261 interval), in Genesis 36:24–37. Incredibly, this word is encoded near the ELS word "Hasmoneans" (-524), which is the name of the family of great warriors led by Judas Maccabaeus. The Hasmonean royal dynasty ruled over Israel and over the Syrians from the time of their victory in 165 B.C. until the Jewish state submitted to the Roman legions of General Pompey in 63 B.C. The name "Mattathias," the man who led the Jewish rebellion against Syria, is also encoded in Genesis 36:33–40 at 62-letter intervals from right to left. In addition, Dr. Doron Witztum, considered by many to be the leading Bible Code researcher, found the name "Maccabee" (which means "hammer") encoded every second letter from right to left in Genesis 36:31–32.

The Assassination of Egyptian President Anwar Sadat

One of the most intriguing series of Bible Codes reveals a tragic event that occurred in our generation—the assassination of Anwar Sadat. The late President Anwar Sadat of Egypt is remembered for his courageous flight to Israel to meet with the Israeli leaders in an attempt to break the circle of continuous warfare between Egypt and Israel that has resulted in waves of violence and bloodshed in the Middle East for decades. Tragically, President Sadat was assassinated in his own country on October 6, 1981 by Islamic fundamentalists from the Moslem Brotherhood, a group who remain violently opposed to the peace process. In Genesis 18, the Israeli researchers found the encoded names "Anwar" and "Sadat" together with the name of the leader of the Moslem Brotherhood assassination team, Chaled Islambooli חאלד אסלמבלי. The assassin's name, חאלד Chaled, is encoded in Genesis 18:4 at 6-letter intervals from right to left, beginning with the second letter of the eighth word in that verse. The same code sequence also contains the day, 8 Tishri (October 6), and the year (1981) of his assassination, along with the following encoded words: president, gunfire, shot, and murder. Incredibly, even the Hebrew word for "parade" appears in this coded sequence. President Sadat was assassinated during his review of a military parade.

The Hitler and Holocaust Codes in the Book of Deuteronomy

The Israeli code researchers naturally wondered if the Bible Codes might reveal anything about the Holocaust, the greatest tragedy in the history of the Jewish people. Their computer search yielded some surprising results. The book of Deuteronomy alone contains two large clusters of encoded words that relate to Hitler and the Holocaust.

When the researchers asked the computer program to search for the target words *Hitler, Nazis,* and *Holocaust,* the computer found that each one of these target words is encoded in a cluster within a small passage in Deuteronomy 10:17–22:

> For the LORD your God is God of gods, and Lord of lords, a great God, a mighty, and a terrible, which regardeth not persons, nor taketh reward: He doth execute the judgment of the fatherless and widow, and loveth the stranger, in giving him food and raiment. Love ye therefore the stranger: for ye were strangers in the land of Egypt. Thou shalt fear the LORD thy God; him shalt thou serve, and to him shalt thou cleave, and swear by his name. He is thy praise, and he is thy God, that hath done for thee these great and terrible things, which thine eyes have seen. Thy fathers went down into Egypt with threescore and ten persons; and now the LORD thy God hath made thee as the stars of heaven for multitude.

First they found the word *Hitler* הישלר spelled out at a 22-letter interval. Several of the names of concentration death camps are found within this same text, beginning with the second to last appearance of the Hebrew letter *bet* ב in this passage. The researchers counted every 13th letter from left to right and discovered that the coded letters spelled out the phrase *b'yam marah Auschwitz,* which means "in the bitter sea of Auschwitz." As they skipped forward another 13 letters, they came to the letter *resh* ר. From the *resh,* they counted every 22nd letter from left to right and connected to the word *Hitler* הישלר, the Jews' greatest enemy.

It was Hitler's satanic hatred of the Jewish people that motivated him to create the Final Solution, which ultimately resulted in the slaughter of over six million Jews and another six million Poles and Russians in the murderous death camps in Eastern Europe. The encoded names of two of the Nazi concentration camps, *Auschwitz* and *Belsen,* are also found close to *Hitler* and *Berlin* in a cluster of encoded words.

Additional Hitler and Holocaust Codes in Deuteronomy

Deuteronomy 31:16–33:21 contains many encoded words referring to Hitler and the Holocaust, including the following: Germany, Poland, genocide, plagues, crematorium, an evil house, and Fuehrer (see list below).

In Deuteronomy 33:16, beginning with the first Hebrew letter *mem* מ, the researchers counted every 246th letter from left to right and found the encoded word *Melek Natzim,* which means "the King of the Nazis." Incredibly, this same passage yielded another hidden code about the rise of Nazi Germany, the phrase *kemi bait rah,* which means "an evil house rose up."

In Deuteronomy 32:52, beginning with the letter *aleph* and counting from left to right every 670 letters spells the name *Aik'man,* a Hebrew variant of the name "Eichmann." Adolf Eichmann was the wicked Nazi official who designed the Final Solution, the evil system of concentration death camps used in the Holocaust. The series of encoded words dealing with Nazi Germany and the Holocaust concludes in Deuteronomy 33:21 with a final astonishing code. Beginning with the letter *resh* ר in the word *Yisrael,* researchers counted every 22nd letter from left to right and found a tragic phrase describing the terrible sufferings of the Jews during the Holocaust: *re'tzach alm,* which means "a people cry murder, slaughter." Many Jews have asked why the prophecies of the Bible say nothing about the Holocaust, the worst tragedy in the history of God's Chosen People. The discovery of the Bible Codes, in the closing years of this century, reveals that God did indeed encode prophetic words about the Holocaust in the Bible.

The Hitler and Holocaust Codes

Encoded Word	Hebrew	Interval	Reference Begins
Hitler	היטלר	(22)	Deut. 10:17
Auschwitz	אושויץ	(-13)	Deut. 10:21
Holocaust	שואה	(13)	Deut. 10:20
Germany Crematorium	גרמניה	(-933)	Deut. 33:28

for my sons	כבשׁן לבני	(134)	Deut. 31:28
The Holocaust	השׁואה	(50)	Deut. 31:16
Plagues	מגפות	(-134)	Deut. 32:32
Eichmann	אייכמן	(670)	Deut. 32:52
Auschwitz	אושׁוויץ	(-536)	Deut. 33:24
In Poland	בפולין	(-107)	Deut. 32:22
King of the Nazis	מלך נאצים	(-246)	Deut. 33:16
Genocide	רצח עם	(-22)	Deut. 33:21
The Fuehrer	הפירר	(5)	Deut. 32:50
Hitler	היטלר	(-3)	Num. 19:13
Mein Kampf	מין קאמפ	(9832)	Num. 22:1

Adolf Hitler, the Nazis, and the Death Camps Were Prophesied in the Bible

היטלר – Hitler

17כי י_וה א_היכם הוא א_הי הא_הים וא_ני הא_נים
הא_ הגדל הגבר והנורא אשר לא-ישא פנים ולא יקח
שחד: 18עשה משפט יתום ואלמנה ואהב גר לתת לו
לחם ושמלה: 19ואהבתם את-הגר כי-גרים הייתם בארץ
מצרים: 20את-י_וה א_היך תירא אתו תעבד ובו תדבק
ובשמו תשבע: 21הוא תהלתך והוא א_היך אשר-עשה
אתך את-הגדלת ואת-הנוראת האלה אשר ראו עיניך:
22בשבעים נפש ירדו אבתיך מצרימה ועתה שמך י_וה
א_היך ככוכבי השמים לרב:

Hebrew text of Deuteronomy 10:17–22

King Louis and the French Revolution

Another passage in the book of Genesis reveals a cluster of encoded words that deal with the French Revolution: "French Revolution" *Mapecha HaSarfatit*(which spells "the French Revolution" in Hebrew); *Louis,* the name of the French king; *Beit* [house of] *Bourbon,* his royal dynasty; *Hamarseilles,* the name of the French national anthem; and *Bastillia,* the infamous French prison for political prisoners that was stormed by revolutionaries. Interestingly, this cluster dealing with the French Revolution appears encoded in Genesis 39–41, the chapters that describe Joseph's imprisonment in Egypt. The Hebrew word for *Bastillia* is found encoded in Genesis 39:20, the verse that describes "the prison in which the king keeps his prisoners."

Ancestors of King David Were Named Centuries before They Were Born

Genesis 38 describes the history of Judah and his daughter-in-law Tamar, who gave birth to Judah's two sons, Pharez and Zerah. The book of Ruth (4:12) tells us that King David, the greatest king of Israel, was descended from Pharez, the son of the patriarch Judah. Pharez was the ancestor of Boaz, who married his kinsman Ruth. They produced a son, Obed, who was the father of Jesse, the father of King David. These five Hebrew names of the key ancestors of King David were found encoded at 49-letter intervals, reading left to right, within the text of Genesis 38. Incredibly, each of these five names is encoded at the same 49-letter interval in the precise chronological order in which the ancestors were born. Dr.

Michelson reported that the odds were only 1 chance in 800,000 that the five names of David's ancestors would occur in this particular passage in the exact chronological order in which they were born.

The Israeli code researchers also examined the text of Genesis 28, a chapter dealing with Jacob's vision of the ladder to heaven, which he received at Mount Moriah, the "place of God." The scientists found the key words "Temple" and "Torah" encoded at 26-letter intervals in a continuous sequence of 9 letters (the combined number of the letters of both Hebrew words). The occurrence of these two significant words occurring together in sequence in a biblical passage that says, "this is none other but the house of God, and this is the gate of heaven" is extraordinary. The researchers calculated that the probability of these key words occurring by chance in a passage about Mount Moriah, the "place of God," is astronomical.

In another analysis, the researchers examined the first chapter of Leviticus, the chapter that records God's laws concerning the priesthood of Aaron, the high priest of Israel. They found the Hebrew name "Aaron" encoded twenty-five times in this one chapter and calculated the odds to be 400,000 to 1 that these codes could occur by chance.

Scientists who have studied the results of the Bible Codes in the Torah conclude that it would be virtually impossible to reproduce this phenomenon in a Hebrew text, even if they had the help of a group of brilliant language geniuses, or the assistance of the world's most sophisticated supercomputers. Moreover, it is impossible to account for the prophetic knowledge of personalities and events found in the codes. The logical conclusion is that God inspired Moses to record the precise Hebrew words in the Torah.

In addition to demonstrating that the text of the Torah was inspired by God, the evidence of such supernatural design destroys the liberal theory that the book of Genesis was created by different "editors" who interwove several different texts centuries after the life of Moses. Only one supernatural mind could have imposed this marvelously complex design upon these five books of the Law. The Israeli researchers also discovered similar codes throughout the whole Old Testament.

As I will reveal in a later chapter, God has provided equally compelling evidence in the Greek text of the New Testament proving that He also inspired the Christian writers to record His precise words to His Church. A number of Christians have asked me why God would have placed a series of hidden codes within the Hebrew Bible and not have placed similar codes within the New Testament. I have been researching the possibility that the Bible Code phenomenon might be found in the Greek text of the New Testament. I funded a small team of computer specialists to develop a computer software program to search the Greek text of the Scriptures. Recently, we discovered a series of Bible Codes about Jesus Christ and various historical events within the Greek New Testament. In a later chapter, I will share this discovery.

The discovery of complex Bible Codes that reveal supernatural and prophetic knowledge about the future has caused tremendous consternation in the academic community. The Bible Code phenomenon challenges the long-held beliefs of liberal scholars, who generally reject the supernatural origin, as well as the verbal inspiration, of the Bible. In 1996, I published my book *The Signature of God*,[5] which analyzed the archeological and scientific evidence that supports the inspiration and authority of the Scriptures. In this book, I presented many Bible Code discoveries, including those discovered by my friend Yacov Rambsel, that reveal the name of Jesus encoded in the messianic passages of the Old Testament. Many Christians throughout the world viewed these code discoveries as powerful new evidence of the inspiration of the Word of God. In the past two years, Rambsel and I have worked together to carefully examine a number of significant codes that will be fascinating to all those who love Jesus Christ. These code discoveries will be presented in a later chapter.

The book of Proverbs contains a fascinating statement suggesting that God sometimes conceals matters from mankind but encourages us to "search out a matter" to fully understand the depths of the Word of God. "It is the glory of God to conceal a matter, but the glory of kings is to search out a matter" (Proverbs 25:2 NASB).

With powerful apologetic evidence such as this, Christians can challenge the skeptics in our generation to consider the claims of the Bible to be the supernatural Word of God. The Lord commands Christians, through the words of Peter in his first epistle, to be prepared to explain and defend the reasonableness of our faith in the Bible and in Jesus Christ: "But sanctify the Lord God in your hearts: and be ready always to give an answer to every man that asketh you a reason of the hope that is in you with meekness and fear" (1 Peter 3:15).

ONE

The Bible Codes Phenomenon

Why Did God Place These Hidden Bible Codes in the Bible?

For almost sixteen centuries, from the time of Emperor Constantine's conversion in A.D. 300 until the beginning of our century, the Bible was generally accepted by Western culture as the inspired and authoritative Word of God. However, during the last hundred years we have witnessed an unrelenting assault on the authority of the Bible by the intellectual elite, the academic community, liberal theologians, and the media. Most people have been exposed to countless attacks on the authority and accuracy of the Scriptures from one or more of these sources.

It would not be surprising, therefore, to discover that God has provided extraordinary new evidence in the form of the Bible Codes to prove to this present, skeptical generation that the Bible is truly the inspired Word of God. The nature of the Bible Codes is so complex that their discovery could not have been possible without the development of high-speed computers that has taken place during the last fifteen years.

In a sense, God secretly hid these incredible codes within the text of the Bible thousands of years ago with a time lock that could not be opened until the arrival of our generation. In His prophetic foreknowledge, God knew that our generation would be characterized by skepticism. In the face of such an unrelenting attack on the authority of the Scriptures, God made a provision in the form of additional scientific evidence that could challenge this modern assault on the Bible.

Significant Bible Codes Versus Accidental ELS Codes

Accidental equidistant letter sequence, or ELS, words, such as "cat" or "dog," can be found in any common text. We can find such words in the pages of any book or even in the daily newspaper, particularly if we are willing to look for ELS words with large equidistant intervals (hundreds or thousands of letters) between the letters that constitute the ELS word. The difference between these random discoveries and the Bible Codes is that the Bible Codes reveal clear evidence of design.

In light of this distinction, it is important to define exactly what constitutes a significant ELS code. Some criteria for establishing legitimate Bible Codes are listed below:

1. A significant number of thematically linked low-interval ELS encoded words that appear clustered together in one or two paragraphs of the biblical text (e.g., thirteen words about the Holocaust and Hitler

in Deuteronomy). Sometimes the ELS words share common letters.

2. A genuine ELS code or a cluster of related ELS codes found at the minimal skip interval within a short Bible passage. This is one of the main criteria used by the Israeli code researchers. The *minimal skip interval* is the lowest ELS interval in which a particular target word is found in the Bible, e.g., every 5 letters. (For example, the name of Jesus is encoded in 1 John 5:13 at 5-letter intervals. This is the smallest ELS skip interval for *Jesus* in the New Testament.)

3. A series of encoded words in a particular text that can be statistically calculated as unlikely or improbable to occur by random chance (e.g., five names of David's ancestors are encoded at 49-letter intervals in Genesis 38).

4. An ELS word encoded in a particular Bible passage that specifically relates to the topic or theme of the encoded word (e.g., "Eden" is encoded sixteen times in a passage about the Garden of Eden in Genesis 2:4–10).

Can We Find This Phenomenon in Other, Nonbiblical Texts?

The following observations can be made regarding ELS words in works other than the Bible:

1. Tests on nonbiblical Hebrew texts, including the Talmud, the Mishneh, and various apocryphal books (sacred books written between the time of the Old

Testament and the New Testament) such as Tobit or First Maccabees, have produced no pattern of significant ELS codes.

2. Examinations of non-Hebrew literature have not revealed significant clusters of ELS codes similar to those that have been found in the Bible.

3. While a single accidental ELS word, such as "Somoza," can be found in any sufficiently long text, such as *War and Peace* or *Moby Dick,* to date no researchers have found any pattern of significant multiple ELS codes relating to prophetic or future events in nonbiblical texts.

The Supreme Care Taken to Copy the Biblical Manuscripts

The Masoretic text was accepted by the Jews as the most accurate of the variant texts that survived throughout the centuries. To copy the biblical text with virtually perfect accuracy century after century required years of training, an extraordinary amount of labor, and the utmost diligence. In addition to the Bible text itself, the Masoretic scribes copied numerous textual notes in the margins of the scrolls. The Synagogue rolls, containing the five books of the Law of Moses (the Pentateuch), were read in the synagogues every Sabbath day. These beautiful, ornate, and very expensive rolls were made with the leather or skins of animals defined as "clean" by the Torah. These carefully prepared skins were then fastened one to another with strings, made also from clean animals, to form a long continuous roll.

The Talmud, which contains detailed commentaries and discussions of every aspect of Jewish Law, reveals precise rules and regulations regarding the preparation of these rolls and the subsequent copying of the sacred text. Nineteenth-century theologian S. Davidson describes this exacting procedure:

A synagogue roll must be written on the skins of clean animals, prepared for the particular use of the synagogue by a Jew. These must be fastened together with strings taken from clean animals. Every skin must contain a certain number of columns, equal throughout the entire codex. The length of each column must not extend over less than forty-eight, or more than sixty, lines; and the breadth must consist of thirty letters. The whole copy must be first lined; and if three words be written in it without a line, it is worthless. The ink should be black, neither red, green, nor any other colour, and be prepared according to a definite recipe. An authentic copy must be the exemplar, from which the transcriber ought not in the least to deviate. No word or letter, not even a yod, must be written from memory, the scribe not having looked at the codex [manuscript] before him. . . . Between every consonant the space of a hair or thread must intervene; between every word the breadth of a narrow consonant; between every new parashah, or section, the breadth of nine consonants; between every book, three lines. The fifth book of Moses must terminate exactly with a line; but the rest need not do so. Besides this, the copyist must sit in full Jewish dress, wash his whole body, not begin to write the name of God with a pen newly dipped in ink, and should a king address him while writing that name he must take no notice of him. . . . The rolls in which these regulations are not observed are condemned to be buried in the ground or burned; or they are banished to the schools, to be used as reading books.[1]

The Biblical Manuscripts Used to Search for Bible Codes

The Israeli researchers use the authorized Masoretic text (also used by Jews worldwide). This text, also known as the Koren text, is read in Jewish synagogues every Sabbath. When the Dead Sea Scrolls were discovered in 1947, scholars were able to examine a treasure trove of ancient biblical manuscripts that contained every one of the books of the Old Testament (except the small book of Esther). When they compared these ancient biblical manuscripts (estimated by scholars to date back to the centuries before the birth of Christ), they were amazed to discover that the present Masoretic text was extremely close to the text found in these Dead Sea Scrolls.

For example, although the five books of Moses contain 304,805 Hebrew letters, the medieval Masoretic text used by the Jews, and by the King James scholars in 1611 to create the Authorized Version of the Bible, differed from the Dead Sea Scrolls text by only 169 letters. While the spelling of some words had changed in the text, the words themselves were remarkably preserved throughout the centuries. This is astonishing when you consider the obvious difficulty of hand copying the hundreds of thousands of individual Hebrew letters that constitute the text of the Old Testament. The discovery of these ancient scrolls provided translators with powerful evidence that God had preserved the integrity of the biblical revelation found in the Holy Scriptures. We can have great confidence that we retain the Word of God today.

Christian scholars around the world usually use the Biblia Hebraica Stuttgartensis (BHS) text of the Hebrew Scriptures in their studies. Although the BHS text follows the Masoretic Koren text quite closely, it varies from it in some of its spelling of biblical words. For example, the BHS text differs from the Masoretic text in 130 letters out of the 304,805 Hebrew letters in the first five books of the Pentateuch, from Genesis to Deuteronomy. While this seems like a very small variation, if the computer is searching for an ELS code in a particular passage of the BHS text where the spelling happens to vary, an individual ELS code may not be found. However, the majority of ELS codes can be found in both the Masoretic Koren text and the BHS text. To the extent that the BHS text varies from the Masoretic text, there is some degree of degradation of the code phenomenon.

Today, very few Hebrew scholars believe that every single letter of the original biblical text has been perfectly preserved from the original manuscripts. However, Orthodox Jews and many conservative Christians do believe that God has preserved the absolute textual accuracy of the Bible. Obviously, to our knowledge, none of the original manuscripts written by the biblical authors has survived.

Some critics have raised the question of whether the Bible Codes phenomenon can be valid if there is any degree of textual variation from the original manuscripts inspired by God. The logical answer to this question is the same as the answer regarding the variations found in the BHS text. To the degree to which any variation in spelling occurred in the

Masoretic text from the original inspired text (if it did), a particular ELS code in that area might be lost. For example, if a letter was actually dropped or added to the text, that subtraction or addition would obviously throw off the original letter count in that passage. However, if a different letter was substituted for the original letter and the ELS code skipped over that letter, the letter count would be preserved and the Bible Code would be unaffected.

Do Vowel Points Affect ELS Intervals?

A number of critics have suggested that because Hebrew can be written with vowel points or, as is more common, without vowel points, the ELS codes cannot be accurate. However, this criticism represents a fundamental misunderstanding about the Hebrew language. Ancient Hebrew and the original biblical Hebrew text consisted entirely of consonants. The vowel sounds were supplied only when speaking or pronouncing the Hebrew words. Tragically, the use of Hebrew in daily life disappeared during the long centuries of Jewish exile among the Gentile nations. Between the sixth and ninth centuries, Jewish scribes began to add vocalization points below and above the Hebrew consonants to assist the reader unfamiliar with Hebrew in correctly pronouncing the words.

Since these vowel points are above or below the consonant, the Hebrew text has an identical number of consonants whether or not vowel points are used. This is why vowel points do not change or modify the number of letters in the Hebrew text and why they do not interfere with the counting of ELS intervals between letters.

Example of Hebrew Text With and Without Vowel Points

Standard Hebrew

הנה ישכיל עבדי ירום ונשא וגבה מאר.

With vowel points

הִנֵּה יַשְׂכִּיל עַבְדִּי יָרוּם וְנִשָּׂא וְגָבַהּ מְאֹד.

While the Hebrew alphabet has twenty-two letters, some of the letters use a variation of form, called a "final form," when they occur at the end of a word. These final-form letters represent the same letter as their corresponding regular form and do not change the meaning of the text. Therefore, Bible Codes analysis (manual or computer) treats the regular and final form of these letters as being identical. This use is very similar to our use of the lower or upper case of a particular letter in English, such as *a* or *A*.

Why Do Some Hebrew Texts Omit
Letters in God's Name?

There is a great reverence for the name of God in Judaism. The holy name of God, YHVH יהוה (called the Tetragrammaton), was only uttered aloud by the high priest of Israel in the Temple in the Holy of Holies on Yom Kippur, the Day of Atonement. To avoid pronouncing the sacred name of God directly, religious Jews use the word *HaShem* השם, meaning "the Name." Moses gave God's command regarding the use of His name in Exodus 20:7: "Thou shalt not take the name of the LORD thy God in vain; for the LORD will not hold him guiltless that taketh his name in vain." In observance of this divine commandment, Jews often substitute the word *Adonai* אדני, which means "Lord." The asterisks and hyphens that appear in the spelling of God's name in Jewish religious texts represent deletions of the letters *lamedh* ל and *heh* ה, letters that are omitted by Orthodox Jews in respect for God's glory when they print His name.

The Encoded Phrase
"Equidistant Letter Sequence" *Shalav A'ot*

In January 1997, I presented the phenomenon of the Bible Codes to a group of academics and Hebrew scholars at a Bible conference held at Tyndale Theological Seminary in Dallas, Texas. I illustrated numerous encoded words from my book *The Signature of God,* including a number of discoveries in the Old Testament of the encoded name of Jesus *(Yeshua)* made by Yacov Rambsel, whom I had invited to the conference. After discussing these codes, Rambsel and I led an in-depth discussion about the method of analysis used in our research. One of the scholars asked if we had discovered any direct reference to the Bible Code phenomenon itself encoded in the Scriptures.

The Hebrew word for "equidistant" is *shalav* שלב, which means either "equally spaced rungs on a ladder" or "several objects equally spaced from one another," such as letters in a text. When Rambsel and I entered the Hebrew word *shalav* שלב into the Torah Codes program on my laptop computer, we were able to report to the group that we had discovered the encoded word "equidistant" *shalav* שלב in every one of the five books of the Torah. The full phrase, "equidistant letter sequence" *shalav a'ot* אות שלב, is also found in the Hebrew text in each book of the Torah.

For example, in the illustration below, found in Genesis 20:2, the phrase appears at equal intervals every 5th letter from right to left. In the following Hebrew verse from the Masoretic text, I have removed the spaces between each word and enlarged every fifth letter to emphasize the Hebrew letters that spell out *hacharak oht shalav,* the Hebrew phrase for "the latticework of the equidistant letter sequence."

ויאמראברהמאלשרהאשׁתואחתיהוא
וישלחאבימלךמלדנלרויקחאתשרה

Genesis *Bereishis* בראשׁית 20:2: "And Abraham said of Sarah, his wife, She is my sister: and Abimelech king of Gerar sent, and took Sarah."

Starting with the enlarged *heh* ה on the second line to the far left and counting every fifth letter from left to right spells *hacharak oht shalav* החרך אות שלב "the latticework of the equidistant letter sequence."

It was fascinating to discover that God has encoded in every one of the five books of the Torah the Hebrew words for "equidistant-letter sequence," *shalav a'ot* אות שלב—the actual phrase used by modern Israeli researchers to describe the Bible Codes phenomenon. This phrase is encoded in the following passages: Genesis 20:2, every 5th letter from left to right; Exodus 35:21–24, every 38th letter from left to right; Leviticus 10:10, every 78th letter from left to right; Numbers 1:45, every 89th letter from left to right; and Deuteronomy 13:19, every 61st letter from left to right.

Passages in the Bible That May Refer to the Bible Codes

There are several passages in the Bible that may hint at the presence of Bible Codes in the Scriptures. Earlier in this book I referred to Proverbs 25:2: "It is the glory of God to conceal a thing: but the honour of kings is to search out a matter." This verse may refer to the fact that God has concealed "a matter" (i.e., the ELS codes) within the Scriptures. Another fascinating passage, describing an angel's prophetic instructions to Daniel regarding the last days, may also refer to the Bible Codes: "But thou, O Daniel, shut up the words, and seal the book, even to the time of the end: many shall run to and fro, and knowledge shall be increased" (Daniel 12:4).

Most Bible scholars agree that the phrase "knowledge shall be increased" refers to the unprecedented explosion of scientific and technological knowledge occurring in our time. Scientists calculate that the total sum of knowledge is now doubling every twenty-four months. However, the phrase "knowledge shall be increased" may also refer to the explosion of knowledge about the Bible Codes occurring in this generation. It is interesting to note that the Hebrew word "computer" is encoded within Daniel 12:4, along with the Hebrew year "5757" (which corresponds to our calendar year September 1996 to September 1997). This was the period when knowledge about the phenomenon of the Bible Codes exploded worldwide.

Another passage in the same chapter of Daniel may also refer to the Bible Codes: "And he said, Go thy way, Daniel: for the words are closed up and sealed till the time of the end" (Daniel 12:9). Since it is obvious that the book of Daniel has been available to be read by Jews, Christians, and anyone else for thousands of years, in what manner were "the words" of Daniel's prophecy "closed up and sealed"? Thousands of books and commentaries about Daniel's prophecies have been written and studied over the centuries by millions of readers. There is probably no other portion of the Bible that has been analyzed as closely as the book of Daniel. Therefore, it is possible that the angel's prophetic words—"the words are closed up and sealed till the time of the end"—may refer to the Bible Codes, which were "closed up and sealed" until our generation, a generation that many believe is "the time of the end."

Are There Mysteries Hidden in the Text of the Bible?

Four times in the Book of Revelation, Jesus Christ refers to Himself as the "Alpha and Omega, the beginning and the ending . . . which is, and which was, and which is to come, the Almighty" (Revelation 1:8). Three additional references to "Alpha and Omega" are found in Revelation 1:11, Revelation 21:6, and Revelation 22:13. "Alpha" is the first letter of the Greek alphabet and "omega" is the last letter. The fourfold repetition of this curious phrase draws our attention to the fact that God has revealed Himself and His plan of redemption for a lost humanity through the medium of the Hebrew and Greek alphabets. This phrase "Alpha and Omega" reminds us that Jesus is the beginning and the end of everything in the universe because He is its Creator. Significantly, Jesus concludes His prophecy in Revelation with this statement: "I am Alpha and Omega, the beginning and the end, the first and the last" (Revelation 22:13).

Many passages in the Bible refer to the significance of the precise letters of the Bible text and to the absolute precision with which God inspired the human writers to record His sacred words. Jesus Christ referred to the inspiration of the Bible in the gospel of Matthew: "For verily I say unto you, Till heaven and earth pass, one jot or one tittle shall in no wise pass from the law, till all be fulfilled" (Matthew 5:18).

Some people have questioned whether there are genuine mysteries hidden in the text of the Holy Scriptures and why God would place such a complex and detailed pattern of encoded words within the text of the Scriptures. Several readers have suggested that the Bible Codes phenomenon cannot be genuine because they assume that all of God's written revelation must be found in the normal surface text of the Word of God.

While His ultimate purposes are beyond the ability of our finite minds to absolutely determine at this point, we can point to a number of parallel examples of hidden patterns of lettering that have been discovered in the Bible. A careful study of the Scriptures reveals that God has indeed hidden some wonderful treasures within the Scriptures that would not be obvious to the casual reader of the Bible.

For example, there are a number of acrostics that appear in the Hebrew text of the Bible that illustrate how God purposely inspired the biblical writers to follow curious and difficult patterns in the writing of His Word. For example, Psalm 119, the longest psalm (and chapter) in the Bible, is a well-known acrostic in which each of the twenty-two sections of that wonderful psalm commences with the appropriate Hebrew letter of the alphabet, beginning with א and ending with the last letter, ת.

Another interesting example of an acrostic pattern is found in Proverbs 31:10–31, the passage about the "virtuous woman" that is read every Sabbath by Orthodox Jewish husbands to their beloved wives. What few people know, however, is that the beginning letter of each verse in this passage makes an acrostic, beginning with the first letter of the Hebrew alphabet, *aleph* א, and proceeding letter by letter through the alphabet.

Another acrostic example is found in Lamentations 1:1–22, the tragic lament of the prophet Jeremiah over the burning of the beautiful Temple and the city of Jerusalem by the Babylonian army. Additional acrostic examples are located in Psalms 9, 10, 25, 34, 37, 111, 112, and 145, as well as in Lamentations 1–4.

While God obviously placed these acrostic textual designs purposely in the text of the Scriptures, many casual readers would read these particular passages without recognizing the complexity of the literary design.

An Example of a Letter Substitution Code in the Bible

The prophecies of Jeremiah provide an example of a different pattern of encoded words. In Jeremiah 25:26, the prophet refers to the king of Babylon as "the king of Sheshach." Jeremiah wrote, "And the king of Sheshach shall drink after them." Historically, there was no king or kingdom known as Sheshach. The prophet actually reversed the

Hebrew letters that spell "Babylon" to write "Sheshach" by using a method of letter substitution in which the first letter of the Hebrew alphabet, *aleph,* is substituted for the last letter of the alphabet, *tav,* and so on, reversing each letter of the whole alphabet. (In English *a* would be substituted for *z, b* for *y, c* for *x,* etc.) This letter-substitution code was called the "permutation of letters" system, or *Atbash,* by the Jewish sages.

Another example of this code is found later in Jeremiah: "How is Sheshach taken! and how is the praise of the whole earth surprised! how is Babylon become an astonishment among the nations!" (Jeremiah 51:41). In this second passage, the prophet's message reveals that the code word "Sheshach" is equivalent to "Babylon."

The *Interpreter's Dictionary of the Bible* refers to Sheshach as follows: "SHESHACH sheshak. KJV translation of שׁשׁך which is probably a cryptogram for BABYLON (so RSV: Jer. 25:26; 51:41)." *The Preacher's Complete Homiletic Commentary* also comments that "the term 'Sheshach' was a disguised name for magnificent Babylon. . . . In the inversion of letters (Sheshach for Babel) there was signified the inverted fortunes of the city."

The last book of the Bible, Revelation, uses another type of code to warn the tribulation believers to count the number of the Beast: "For it is the number of a man; and his number is Six hundred threescore and six"(13:18). Thus the Bible clearly refers to the system of calculating a name by the numerical value of its letters.

TWO

The Ancient Discovery of the Bible Codes

While the phenomenon of the Bible Codes has taken the world by storm in the last two years, the truth is that many individuals in past centuries had already discovered and documented the existence of Bible Codes.

Rabbi Bachya and the Codes

Six hundred years ago, Rabbi Bachya, a European rabbi, wrote a book in which he described his discovery of a pattern of letters that formed meaningful words encoded in the Torah at equally spaced intervals. When he examined the Hebrew letters, beginning in Genesis 1:1, he noticed that if he began with the last letter (*tav* ת) in the first word of the Bible—*Bereishis* בראשית "beginnings"—and skipped every 49 letters, the word *Torah* תורה was spelled out. In other words, every 50th letter of the text spelled the word *Torah* תורה.

Rabbi Bachya also found that the opening verse of Exodus contained the word *Torah* תורה, also spelled out at the same 50-letter interval, beginning with the first appearance of the

THE MYSTERIOUS BIBLE CODES

letter ה. When he examined the opening verses of Leviticus, however, he could not find the encoded word *Torah* תורה. Instead, he discovered the Hebrew word *HaShem*, which means "the Name" (of God), spelled out every 8th letter, beginning with the first letter, *yod* י.

When the rabbi examined the initial verses of Numbers and Deuteronomy, the fourth and fifth books of the Bible, again he found that the word *Torah* תורה was encoded. In the book of Numbers, *Torah* תורה was spelled out in reverse at a 50-letter interval and in Deuteronomy, to his surprise, *Torah* תורה was spelled out in reverse order at a 49-letter interval, beginning with the fifth verse.

Dr. Daniel Michelson calculated that, based on a letter-frequency analysis, the odds are more than 3 million to 1 against the word *Torah* תורה being encoded by chance, beginning within the first word of Genesis. Therefore, the odds that the word *Torah* תורה would appear in ELS code at the very beginning of each of the four books of Moses simply by chance are astronomical.

References to the Codes in Ancient Jewish Writings

There is a Jewish tradition that a number of Bible Codes were discovered in past centuries by various sages, including Rabbi Nachmanides, Rabbi Bachya, and the Vilna Gaon.

The great Rabbi Nachmanides (known as "Ramban") referred to the code phenomenon in several of his writings. In the introduction to his famous commentary on the Torah, Rabbi Nachmanides wrote that the phenomenon of hidden divine names encoded in every letter of the Torah provided another powerful reason to guard the integrity and perfection of every letter of the biblical text. He taught that a Torah scroll should be considered as unfit for use if even one single letter was missing from the text. The removal or addition of a single letter from the Hebrew text of the Scriptures would eliminate the codes found hidden within that particular section of text.

The Jewish Talmud contains an interesting reference suggesting that "everything is alluded to in the Torah. . . . Rabbi Johanan thereupon exclaimed in amazement: Is there anything written in the Hagiographa to which allusion cannot be found in the Torah?" (*Ta'anis* 9a).

A curious reference to the *Atbash* letter-substitution code found in Jeremiah 25:26 also appears in the Talmud: "To have future events revealed, occasionally letters from words must be read in reverse" (*Yeshayahu* 41:23). Other references to the existence of the Bible Codes can be found in passages in the following ancient Jewish writings and commentaries: *Zohar* 2:161a; *B'reishis Rabah* 1:1; *Tanchuma* 1:1; *Raya M'hemna;* and *B'reishis* 23a.

Centuries ago a famous sage, known as Rabbi Moses Cordevaro, spoke about the existence of these codes: "For the number of things that one can discover in the Torah via certain methods is without limit—infinite. Such matters are enormously powerful, and very deeply hidden. Because of how they are hidden it is not possible to comprehend them fully, but only in part." Interestingly, Rabbi Cordevaro also spoke directly about the "secrets of the Torah" being hidden in "the skipping of letters."[1]

Louis Ginzberg edited a tremendous compilation of ancient traditions of the Jewish people in his seven-volume encyclopedia, *The Legends of the Jews,* which contains several references to the existence of Bible Codes:[2]

God had revealed to him [Moses] the treasures of the Torah, of wisdom, and of knowledge, and the whole world's future. (vol. 2, p. 324)

. . . the secret of the Holy Names as they are contained in the Torah, and as they are applied. (vol. 3, p. 114)

In this book he found recorded all the generations from the creation of the world to the resurrection of the dead, and the kings, leaders, and prophets set down beside every generation. (vol. 3, p. 154)

The *Zohar* and the Bible Codes

An intriguing statement about divine names existing in coded form within the Scriptures can be found in the ancient Jewish mystical book known as the *Zohar:* "The whole Torah is filled with Divine Names. Divine Names run through every word in the Torah" (*Zohar* 2:87a).

The *Zohar* also contains a reference to the rediscovery of the Bible Codes in our generation:

Rabbi Yose entered a cave and found in it a book which was stuck into a cleft in the rock at the far end of a cave. He brought it out, and when he opened it, he saw the shapes of seventy-two letters which were given to Adam the first man, and through which Adam knew all the wisdom of the Supernal Holy Beings and of all those who [sit] behind the millstones that turn behind the Veil of the Supernal Lights, and [knew] all the things that were to come to pass in the world until the day when a cloud that is on the west side would arise and cast darkness upon the world. Rabbi Yose called Rabbi Y'huda, and they began to study the book. But as soon as they had studied two or three pages of those letters, they found themselves looking at that Supernal Wisdom. When they came to delve into the mysteries of the book, and began to discuss them among themselves, a fiery flame and a gust of wind came and struck their hands, and the book disappeared.

Rabbi Yose wept and said: "Perhaps, God forbid, we are guilty of sin, or is it that we are not worthy to know these things?" When they came to Rabbi Shim'on and told him what had happened, he said to them: "Perhaps you were trying to learn about the Messianic end from those letters?" They said to him: "That we do not know, for we have forgotten all of it." Rabbi Shim'on said to them: "it is not the will of the Holy One, blessed be He, that too much be revealed to the world. But when the days of the Messiah approach, even the children of the world will be able to discover secrets of wisdom, and to know through them the Ends and the Calculations, and in that time it will be revealed to all." (1:117b–18a)

This statement in the *Zohar* seems to imply that in the last days "even the children of the world will be able to discover the secrets of wisdom" and will discover information about "the Ends and the Calculations." Since a bright child with a desktop computer and the appropriate Bible Codes software program can search the Scriptures for Bible Codes, is it possible that this statement implies the rediscovery of the phenomenon of the Bible Codes in our generation? Where would the authors of the *Zohar* have found the idea that the generation that lives in the last days would discover these hidden codes? The prophecy of Daniel 12:4 clearly suggests such an idea: "But thou, O Daniel, shut up the words, and seal the book, even to the time of the end: many shall run to and fro, and knowledge shall be increased."

The Date of the Writing of the *Zohar*

Many Jewish and Christian scholars have suggested that the *Zohar* was actually written by Rabbi Moses de Leon in the fourteenth century. However, the text of the *Zohar* itself declares that it was composed by Rabbi Simon bar Yochai during the first century of the Christian era, approximately two thousand years ago. In 1997, Dr. Jeffrey Satinover wrote about this literary controversy and its possible resolution in his excellent book *Cracking the Bible Codes*.[3]

Rabbi Yitzchak deMin Acco was a fourteenth-century Jewish scholar who lived in the same century as Rabbi Moses de Leon. He investigated the authorship of the *Zohar* because there were many rumors at the time that his contemporary, Rabbi Moses de Leon, had secretly composed the book. According to the book *Sefer HaYuchasin*, Rabbi Yitzchak deMin Acco's written account of his investigation of the true authorship of the *Zohar* ends abruptly, just before he was about to announce his conclusion regarding this question. However, many modern scholars, while admitting that Rabbi Yitzchak deMin Acco's conclusions are unknown, have announced their own conclusions. They reject the claim that the *Zohar* was written by Rabbi Simon bar Yochai in the first century of this era, based on evidence from medieval sources far removed in time from the claimed date of authorship.

Fortunately, in 1976 the scholar Rabbi Aryeh Kaplan obtained a photocopy of the sole surviving manuscript of Rabbi Yitzchak deMin Acco's study, known as *Otzar HaChaim*. Rabbi Kaplan found this extremely rare fourteenth-century manuscript at the Lenin Library in Moscow amidst a huge collection of ancient Hebrew texts that the Soviet government had acquired from Jewish libraries and synagogues during the years of Soviet domination of Eastern Europe. It was hidden among other manuscripts in the Gunzberg Judaica Collection.

Rabbi Yitzchak deMin Acco's investigation of Rabbi Moses de Leon concluded that, based on overwhelming literary and historical evidence, the *Zohar* was actually created by the traditionally claimed author, Rabbi Simon bar Yochai, in the first century, almost two millennia ago. Rabbi Kaplan presented his conclusion that the *Zohar* was a genuine ancient Jewish text in a report entitled "Kabbalah and the Age of the Universe," which he delivered in a speech to the Midwinter Conference of the Association of Orthodox Jewish Scientists on February 19, 1976.[4]

The Vilna Gaon and the Bible Codes

Several centuries ago, the famous Rabbi Eliyahu ben Shlomo (1797), known as the Vilna Gaon, lived and taught in the city of Vilna, Latvia, near the Baltic Sea in northern Europe. This brilliant, mystical Jewish sage taught his yeshiva (Jewish Bible School) students that God had hidden and secretly encoded a vast amount of information within the Hebrew letters of the Torah. Consider the Vilna Gaon's fascinating and suggestive statement in the introduction to *Sifra Ditzniut* about the hidden codes:

The rule is that all that was, is, and will be unto the end of time is included in Torah from the first word to the last word. And not merely in a general sense, but including the details of every species and of each person individually, and the most minute details of everything that happened to him from the day of his birth until his death; likewise of every kind of animal and beast and living thing that exists, and of herbage, and of all that grows or is inert.

From these historical references, it is certain that the mystery of the hidden Bible Codes was known to some of the wisest of the Jewish sages through their lifelong devotion to the Holy Scriptures. Considering how difficult it is to detect ELS codes without using a computer program, one can only marvel at the tremendous dedication and scholarship of these men.

Sir Isaac Newton, possibly the greatest scientist in history, was fascinated with the Bible and prophecy. Although he wrote extensively about science, very few people realize that he actually wrote more about theology than he did about science. He was provost of Cambridge University in England until 1696 and wrote a fascinating book called *Observations on Daniel and the Revelation.* John Maynard Keynes, also a provost at Cambridge earlier in this century, discovered a treasure of unpublished writings that Newton had left at the university.

In the course of writing Newton's biography, Keynes sifted through his voluminous writings and was astonished to learn that Newton spent most of his time writing about obscure aspects of theology, including prophecy. However, Keynes's biggest surprise was the number of manuscripts he discovered that evidenced Newton's near obsession with finding a secret letter code hidden within the Hebrew text of the Holy Scriptures. While he never found the key to the Bible Codes, Newton apparently intuitively recognized that there had to be a series of encoded words in the Bible.

Although various individuals throughout the history of the last two thousand years have found occasional code words, it was not until this century that Bible Code research made real progress. The creation of sophisticated high-speed computers and software programs that enable the search of the Bible's text at thousands of calculations per second allowed researchers to discover the vast number of complex ELS codes that were hidden within the sacred text of the Holy Scriptures.

THREE

The Rediscovery of the Bible Codes in Modern Times

Rabbi Weissmandl's Astonishing Discovery

Rabbi Michael Dov Weissmandl was a brilliant Czechoslovakian Jewish scholar in astronomy, mathematics, and Judaic studies who made some phenomenal discoveries during the turbulent years leading to World War II. Rabbi Weissmandl found an obscure reference to these codes in a book written by a fourteenth-century rabbi, Rabbeynu Bachayah. This reference described a pattern of letters encoded within the Torah, the first five books of the Bible. This report inspired Rabbi Weissmandl to search for other examples of codes hidden within the Torah. He located certain meaningful words, phrases, and word pairs, such as "hammer" and "anvil," by finding the first letter of the target word and then skipping forward a certain number of letters to find the second one, and an equal number again to find the third one, and so on. For example, he found the letter *tav* ת, the first letter of the word *Torah* תורה, the Hebrew word for "law," within the first word of Genesis 1:1, "Beginnings" *Bereishis* בראשית. Then, by skipping forward 50 letters, he found the second letter *vav* ו. He continued to skip forward 50 letters and found *reysh* ר and finally the last letter *hey* ה, completing the spelling of the word *Torah* תורה. The rabbi was astonished to find that many significant words were hidden within the text of the Torah at equally spaced intervals. These intervals varied from every 2 letters up to hundreds of letters apart.

Although Rabbi Weissmandl found many encoded names, he did not record his code discoveries in writing. Fortunately, some of his Jewish students did. Over the following decades, students in Israel who had heard about his research began searching the Torah for themselves to ascertain whether or not such codes actually existed. Their discoveries ultimately resulted in research studies at Hebrew University that have proven the validity of the codes, now known as equidistant letter sequence (ELS) codes. In the last thirteen years, the introduction of sophisticated high-speed computers has allowed Jewish scholars at Hebrew University to explore the text of the Torah in ways that were unavailable to previous generations. In 1988 three mathematics and computer experts at Hebrew University and the Jerusalem College of Technology (Dr. Doron Witztum, Dr. Yoav Rosenberg, and Dr. Eliyahu Rips) completed a fascinating research project that followed up Rabbi Weissmandl's original research.

The Process of Analyzing the Hebrew Text of the Bible

Using the ancient Hebrew textus receptus (the Masoretic text or Koren text) of the Torah, the team of Israeli researchers at

Hebrew University began their systematic search for Bible Codes by first eliminating all the spaces between the Hebrew letters, words, and sentences of the Torah, the first five books of the Bible. The traditional orthodox text was originally written without punctuation marks or spaces between letters, words, grammatical marks, or sentences. To demonstrate what such a text would look like, let us take a sentence in English and write it out as it would appear in an ancient Hebrew manuscript.

THEBIBLEWASWRITTENINHEBREWWITHOUT-
PUNCTUATIONMARKS

With spaces, this sentence would read as follows:

THE BIBLE WAS WRITTEN IN HEBREW WITHOUT
PUNCTUATION MARKS.

In the writings of the ancient Jewish sages there is a curious tradition that claims that Moses had a vision on Mt. Sinai in which the Hebrew letters of the Torah appeared to him as letters of black fire in a continuous sequence without spaces against a background of white fire. The sages wrote that Moses recorded these divinely revealed letters one by one, spelling out the five books of God's Law called the Torah.

The Three Hundred Word-Pairs Experiment

As mentioned earlier, in 1988 three mathematics and computer experts at Hebrew University and the Jerusalem College of Technology (Dr. Doron Witztum, Dr. Yoav

Rosenberg, and Dr. Eliyahu Rips) published the results of a unique research project that followed up on Rabbi Weissmandl's original research conducted in the 1940s. The results of the researchers' initial experiment appeared as part of a larger article dealing with statistics and theology in a 1988 issue of the *Journal of the Royal Statistical Society.*

In their experiment the scientists arbitrarily chose 300 Hebrew word pairs that were logically related in meaning, such as *hammer* and *anvil,* or *tree* and *leaf,* or *man* and *woman.* They asked the computer program to locate any such word pairs in the Hebrew text of Genesis. Once the computer found the first Hebrew letter of *hammer,* for example, it would look for the second letter at various intervals between the letters. If the program could not locate the second letter of the target word *hammer* following the first letter at a 2-space interval, it would then search at a 3-space interval, then a 4-space interval, et cetera. Once it located the second letter at, for example, a 12-space interval, it would then look for the third letter at the same 12-space interval, and so on through the entire 78,064 Hebrew letters in the book of Genesis.

The computer also looked for coded words by checking in reverse order. Since the computer can compute millions of calculations per second, the scientists could quickly examine every 4th, 5th, 6th, 7th letter, for example. The sophisticated computers could examine every one of millions of possible combinations to discover encoded words that no human could have ever found manually. The only limitation was the imagination of the researchers to think of target words to search for, such as *Hitler, Berlin,* or *Sadat.*

When the computer program finished examining the text for each of the 300 word-pairs, the researchers were intrigued to realize that every single word-pair had been located in Genesis in close proximity to its mate. As mathematical statisticians, they were naturally amazed because they knew it was humanly impossible to construct such an intricate and complicated pattern in a text of literature such as Genesis, much of which is the history of the Jewish people. After calculating the astronomical probabilities that this phenomenon could occur randomly by chance alone, they published their experiment as part of a larger article dealing with statistics and theology in a 1988 issue of the British *Journal of the Royal Statistical Society.*[1]

Unfortunately, there has been a great deal of unnecessary controversy and misinformation about the article that reported the results of the researchers' experiment. Dr. Jeffrey Satinover reported on the 1988 article in an article in *Bible Review,*[2] and I referred to it in my book *The Signature of God.* When a number of critics checked directly with the Royal Statistical Society, the office stated that they had not published any articles by Drs. Witztum, Rosenberg, and Rips. Without contacting me for clarification, Jewish and Christian critics alike attacked my credibility publicly on the Internet and in published articles, claiming I was either carelessly inaccurate or had falsely made up the reference.

However, the truth is that Dr. Satinover and I are correct. Drs. Witztum, Rosenberg, and Rips did in fact write a report on their research, which was published in the 1988 publication that we cited. Two factors have caused the misunderstanding. First, the Israeli researchers' portion of the paper dealing with the Bible Codes appeared in the final part of a larger paper entitled "Probability, Statistics and Theology." That paper, which was read before the Royal Statistical Society at the London School of Economics and Political

Science in England on November 11, 1987, and published in the *Journal of the Royal Statistical Society,* was written by D. J. Bartholomew.[3]

The second factor that led to the misunderstanding about this 1988 article was the fact that when Drs. Witztum, Rosenberg, and Rips later submitted their detailed study on the "Famous Rabbis" experiment (explained below) in an article entitled "Equidistant Letter Sequences in the Book of Genesis," this extraordinary scientific article was rejected by the Royal Statistical Society on the basis that it did not fit its scholarly criteria. Therefore, when asked, their office naturally issued denials that they had ever published the "Equidistant Letter Sequences in the Book of Genesis" article. This is why the critics were confused. The critics asked the wrong question. If they had asked to examine the 1988 article Dr. Satinover and I cited, they would have found confirmation of the information we referred to. To finally settle this matter I personally visited the Royal Statistical Society's office in London to obtain a copy of the article from their editor. The portion of the 1988 article in the *Journal of the Royal Statistical Society* dealing with the Israeli researchers' earlier experiment on ELS Codes in Genesis is quoted in the appendix of this book.

The Bible Codes Reveal the Names of Sixty-Six Famous Rabbis

For six years the Israeli researchers found that various scientific journals would not agree to publish their experiment, despite the fact that the ELS code research and statistical conclusions were impressive. Finally, in August 1994, the

American journal *Statistical Science,* one of the most prominent mathematical and scientific journals in the world, published their research on the "Famous Rabbis" experiment in
an article entitled "Equidistant Letter Sequences in the Book
of Genesis." Drs. Witztum, Rosenberg, and Rips completed
the research for this article at Hebrew University and the
Jerusalem College of Technology. Their research on the ELS
codes has been documented in several scholarly journals in
both Israel and America, including *Bible Review* (Oct.
1995), and on many Web sites on the Internet.

In the "Famous Rabbis" experiment, the Israeli researchers
recorded the results of their search for pairs of encoded words
that reveal the names and dates of births or deaths of a group
of famous Jewish rabbis who lived thousands of years after the
time Moses wrote the Torah. The team initially selected the
names of thirty-four of the most prominent rabbis and Jewish
sages during the thousand years from A.D. 90 to A.D. 1900. The
researchers simply selected the thirty-four sages with the
longest biographies in the *Encyclopedia of Great Men in
Israel,*[4] a well-respected Hebrew reference book.

They asked the computer program to search the text of
Genesis for close ELS word pairs coded at equally spaced
intervals that contained the name of a famous rabbi paired
with his date of birth or death (using the Hebrew month and
day). The Jewish people celebrate the memory of a famous
sage by commemorating his date of death. The researchers
found that every one of the thirty-four names of the famous
rabbis encoded in Genesis is paired at significantly close
proximity to the date of the particular rabbi's birth or death.
The odds that these particular names and dates could occur
in close proximity by random chance were calculated by the
mathematicians to be only 1 chance in 775 million.

Some critics have suggested that the Israeli scientists simply played with the computer program long enough, until by chance alone, "they got lucky." This criticism raises the relevant objection that there might be numerous unreported "hidden failures," a common problem in most scientific research today. To eliminate the possibility that this had occurred, *Statistical Science* demanded that the scientists analyze their data by examining a completely new group of personalities of the *Statistical Science* editorial judges' own choosing. The judges requested the second sample be taken from the next thirty-two most prominent Jewish sages listed in the encyclopedia. In addition, the judges appointed by *Statistical Science* analyzed the computer programs to determine that they were both valid and neutral in their design.

To the surprise of the skeptical reviewers, the results of the second set of famous Jewish sages were equally successful. The outcome of the combined test revealed that the names and dates of the birth or death of each one of the sixty-six most famous Jewish sages were encoded in pairs in close proximity in the text of Genesis. Despite the fact that all of the journal's reviewers held previous beliefs against the inspiration of the Scriptures, the overwhelming evidence and the integrity of the data forced the editors to approve the study's scientific accuracy and reluctantly publish the article.

Robert Kass, the editor of *Statistical Science,* wrote this comment about the study: "Our referees were baffled: their prior beliefs made them think the Book of Genesis could not possibly contain meaningful references to modern day individuals, yet when the authors carried out additional analyses and checks the effect persisted. The paper is thus offered to *Statistical Science* readers as a challenging puzzle."[5]

An article in *Bible Review* magazine (Oct. 1995) by Dr. Satinover reported that the mathematical probability of the names of sixty-six Jewish sages, paired with the dates of their birth or death, occurring by random chance in an ancient text like Genesis was less than 1 chance in 2.5 billion. Interestingly, when the researchers attempted to duplicate these ELS codes by analyzing other religious Hebrew texts, such as the Talmud, the Mishneh, and the Samaritan Pentateuch, the researchers failed to find codes of any significance. The duplicate experiment on the Samaritan Pentateuch is especially noteworthy considering that this religious work is a variant text of the five books of Moses that differs in numerous small textual details from the Masoretic text of the Hebrew Bible.

Following the appearance of Dr. Satinover's October 1995 article in *Bible Review,* the magazine received an onslaught of letters to the editor that attacked the article in the strongest terms. Most of the critical letters dismissed the phenomenon outright, without seriously considering the scientific data that was presented. Several critics attacked Dr. Satinover's argument and data in ways that revealed that they either failed to grasp the actual statistical method used to detect the Bible Codes or didn't understand the rigorous methodology that eliminated the possibility that this phenomenon had occurred by pure random chance.

Dr. Satinover responded to his critics in the February 1996 issue of *Bible Review:*

> The robustness of the Bible Codes findings derives from the rigor of the research. To be published in a journal such as *Statistical Science,* it had to run, without stumbling, an

unusually long gauntlet manned by some of the world's most eminent statisticians. The results were thus triply unusual: in the extraordinariness of what was found; in the strict scrutiny the findings had to hold up under; and in the unusually small odds (less than 1 in 62,500) that they were due to chance.

Other amazing claims about the Bible, Shakespeare, etc., have never even remotely approached this kind of rigor, and have therefore never come at all close to publication in a peer-reviewed, hard-science venue. The editor of *Statistical Science,* himself a skeptic, has challenged readers to find a flaw. Though many have tried, none has succeeded. All the "First Crack" questions asked by *Bible Review* readers—and many more sophisticated ones—have therefore already been asked by professional critics and exhaustively answered by the research. Complete and convincing responses to even these initial criticisms can get fairly technical.[6]

A Master Pentagon Code Breaker Verifies the Bible Codes

Professor Harold Gans, a brilliant mathematician who has published over one hundred eighty technical papers, was a senior researcher with the National Security Agency. Professor Gans's job at the NSA was to examine sophisticated foreign government intelligence codes for the Pentagon. Dr. Gans has publicly confirmed the existence of the Bible Codes, as reported in *Statistical Science,* by using advanced analytic techniques and his own computer program. When he first learned of the discovery of the Bible

Codes, as a skeptic and nonbeliever, he initially believed that the claims were "ridiculous." However, as an intelligence specialist dealing with complex codes and computers, Gans had the technical ability to test the claims and the data for himself. In 1989, he created a complex, original computer program to check Drs. Witztum, Rosenberg, and Rips's data.

For nineteen days and nights, Gans let his program examine all possible variations and combinations in the 78,064 Hebrew letters in the book of Genesis. Dr. Gans's computer program checked through hundreds of thousands of possible letter combinations at many differently spaced intervals. Finally, Gans concluded that these Bible Codes actually existed and that they could not occur by chance or by human design. He had confirmed the absolute accuracy of Drs. Witztum, Rosenberg, and Rips's conclusions. Because of his discoveries, Dr. Gans now teaches classes in synagogues throughout the world, sharing the incredible evidence that proves the divine authorship of the Bible.

Dr. Gans completed a follow-up study and discovered that encoded names of the cities where each of these sixty-six sages was born are also encoded in the book of Genesis. Drs. Witztum, Rosenberg, and Rips produced a new scientific paper based on this additional data about the cities of birth of the sages and calculated that the odds that this could occur by chance alone were 1 chance in 250 million.

In response to the claim of the critics that this phenomenon is a result of simple chance, the Israeli code researchers calculated that the odds of even one of these codes occurring by chance (i.e., a rabbi's name, date of birth or death, and the city where he was born) are only 1 chance in 62,500. It is important to remember that most science journals accept a phenomenon as being significant if the odds against the event

THE MYSTERIOUS BIBLE CODES

occurring by chance are greater than 1 in 100. However, when we examine the series of complex ELS patterns mentioned in this book, the probability is astronomical that these Bible Codes have been placed in the Scriptures by divine purpose.

The Response to the Codes from Recognized Mathematical Experts

The well-respected mathematician Dr. David Kazhdan, chairman of the mathematics department at Harvard University, and his fellow scientists from Yale and Hebrew University in Jerusalem, have confirmed that this is "serious research carried out by serious investigators." Dr. Kazhdan warned against casually rejecting the evidence of the Bible Codes: "The phenomenon is real. What conclusion you reach from this is up to the individual."

A group of recognized experts in mathematics, including Dr. Kazhdan, wrote a letter confirming the value of this research in the introduction to a recent Israeli book about this phenomenon called *Maymad HaNosaf (The Added Dimension)*, written by Dr. Witztum, now considered by many to be the leading researcher on these Bible Codes. Realizing that this discovery is extremely controversial in today's academic world, these scientists encouraged additional research on the phenomenon. The letter in the introduction to *Maymad HaNosaf* follows:

Statement on the Validity of the Research of Witztum, Rips and Rosenberg
Doron Witztum, together with his collaborators,

Professor Ilya Rips and Yoav Rosenberg, have attempted to study the phenomenon systematically aided by high-speed computers. The goal of their research has been to establish that the phenomenon in question is a real one, i.e. that its prevalence cannot be explained purely on the basis of fortuitous combinations.

Following this procedure the author and his collaborators make a rather convincing case for the predominance of equally spaced occurrences of "meaningful" word pairs. Finally, to provide as objective a criterion as possible for the relatedness of word pairs, the author with his collaborators describe an experiment with particularly interesting results in which they study this proximity measure for names of prominent Jewish figures together with dates of demise of these figures. The present work represents serious research carried out by serious investigators. Since the interpretation of the phenomenon in question is enigmatic and controversial, one may want to demand a level of statistical significance beyond what would be demanded for more routine conclusions. While it is premature to say that the author's thesis has been established decisively, the results obtained are sufficiently striking to deserve a wide audience and to encourage further study.

> *Professor H. Furstenberg,*
> the Hebrew University of Jerusalem,
> *Professor I. Piatetski-Shapiro,*
> Tel Aviv University and Yale University,
> *Professor David Kazhdan,*
> Harvard University,
> *Professor J. Bernstein,*
> Harvard University.[7]

FOUR

Some Cautions about Bible Codes

As with many other kinds of biblical studies, the Bible Code discoveries are open to misunderstanding and vulnerable to misuse. Therefore, to preserve the integrity of legitimate Bible Codes it is important to establish some parameters about the use and misuse of Bible Codes.

Bible Codes Cannot Be Used to Accurately Foretell Future Events

Aside from the fact that the Bible specifically prohibits us from engaging in fortune-telling, it is not possible to discover meaningful encoded information about a future event until the event has occurred. It would be impossible to know what target word to ask the program to search for. Moreover, even if you correctly guessed at the right target words for a future event (e.g., the assassination of a prominent politician) and you found the name of the person along with the word "killed," you would still not know anything certain about the future. Until the event occurs, any suggestion that the occurrence of these two code words means that the politician will be killed would be merely a guess. However, once an event occurs, such as the War in the Gulf, we can ask the computer to look in the Bible text for such target words as "Saddam Hussein" or "General Schwarzkopf."

In other words, the Bible Codes can confirm that the Scriptures contain encoded data about historical events that occurred centuries after the Scriptures were written, but they cannot be used to foretell future events. The major Israeli code researchers, including Dr. Eliyahu Rips, and all of the serious Christian researchers deny that the Bible Codes can be used to accurately predict future events. The information encoded in the Bible can only be accurately interpreted after a historical event has actually occurred. Then, we can compare the details of the historical event with the encoded information in the Bible to determine whether God had encoded these prophetic details centuries before the events occurred. In this manner, the Bible Codes give God the glory, not the human researcher. The prophet Isaiah declared these words of God: "I will not give my glory unto another" (Isaiah 48:11).

Bible Codes Do Not Reveal Any Hidden Theological Sentences, Teachings, or Doctrines

There are no secret sentences, detailed messages, or theological statements in the encoded words. God's message of salvation and His commandments for holy living are found only in the open text of the Scriptures. The Bible Codes only reveal key words—such as names, places, and, occasionally, dates (using the Hebrew calendar)—that can be used as evidence to confirm the supernatural inspiration and origin of the Scriptures.

The Bible Codes Have Nothing to Do with Numerology

The phenomenon of the Bible Codes has nothing to do with numerology. Numerology is defined by the authoritative *Webster's Dictionary* as "the study of the occult significance of numbers." Numerology is connected with divination or foretelling the future and is clearly forbidden by the Bible. There is nothing occult or secret about the codes. The Bible Code phenomenon has been openly published in scientific and mathematical journals and taught throughout the world since it was first discovered thirteen years ago.

The particular skip interval (the actual number of letters to be skipped) between Hebrew letters has no importance or significance. The codes have nothing to do with "the occult significance of numbers." Obviously, the encoded words are found at various intervals (e.g., by skipping 2, 7, 61, or more letters). However, the significance or meaning of the encoded word has no relationship to the particular interval (the number of letters skipped). Either a particular word is spelled out in Hebrew letters at equal intervals or it is not. Anyone can examine a particular encoded word to verify that these words are spelled out at ELS intervals. Computer programs such as the Bible Codes are publicly available on the Internet or from ministries such as my own to assist in the process of verification.

A Caution about Michael Drosnin's Book *The Bible Code*

The Bible Code, a book written by Michael Drosnin and published in the late spring of 1997, caused a great sensation in the Christian community and in the secular community.[1] Although several books on this topic had been published prior to Drosnin's book (including my book, *The Signature of God*, and the books of several Israeli authors), *The Bible Code* was extensively promoted by its publisher in virtually every major media outlet from CNN to *TIME* magazine to "The Oprah Winfrey Show." As a result, the whole world is now talking about the Bible Codes. On balance, I believe this publicity has been positive in that it has created a curiosity about the phenomenon in the minds of tens of millions of readers who would otherwise never have read about the Bible Codes. Perhaps God will use Drosnin's secular approach to the Bible Codes to draw many people into a closer examination of the Bible with the result that many will be introduced to Jesus Christ.

Naturally, I have received many letters and questions on radio talk shows about my response to *The Bible Code*. While Drosnin reports many new and exciting discoveries made by Israeli code researchers such as Dr. Rips, he does so, unfortunately, from a position somewhere between atheism and agnosticism. While he admits that only a supernatural being could have produced the Bible Codes thirty-five hundred years ago, Drosnin firmly rejects the conclusion that the author is God.

The Problem with Drosnin's Predictions

A much greater objection to Drosnin's book is his false claim that the Bible Codes can be used to accurately predict future events. One of his major claims is that he personally discovered the encoded word "Yitzchak Rabin." The first letter of Rabin's name begins in Deuteronomy 2:33, and the second letter is found 4,772 letters forward in the text of Deuteronomy 4:42, a passage that contains the words "will be assassinated." In the King James Bible this phrase is translated, "kill his neighbour unawares." Upon making this discovery, Drosnin claims that he flew to Israel to warn Prime Minister Rabin of his imminent danger. Although I read Israeli newspapers regularly and follow Israeli events daily on the Internet, I have yet to see any of the prime minister's staff confirm that this warning was actually given to Rabin. Therefore, it is difficult to evaluate Drosnin's claim.

Nevertheless, if Drosnin actually flew to Israel to warn the prime minister, based solely on the fact that he found the second letter of Rabin's name in the phrase "will be assassinated" in Deuteronomy 4:42, he did so simply because he had made a leap of presumption. How could Drosnin know, in advance of the event, that this code actually meant that Rabin would be assassinated? I do not deny that the code is significant. That is why I wrote about the "Rabin" code in my earlier book. However, in advance of the tragic event, it was impossible to know that the encoded word meant that the assassination would definitely occur. The most Drosnin could do was make a guess. He certainly would have been aware of the increasing number of public threats Rabin received in letters to newspapers and on signs held up at political rallies in the year preceeding the assassination. But why would Drosnin become so convinced—to the point of flying to Israel to warn Rabin—simply because one of the eight encoded letters of Rabin's name occurred in the phrase "will be assassinated"?

How could anyone know, in advance of the assassination, that the phrase "will be assassinated" was significant, as opposed to all of the other phrases that contained the remaining letters of Rabin's name, which stretched throughout the book of Deuteronomy at intervals of 4,772 letters? For example, the first letter of the encoded name "Yitzchak Rabin" is found in the first word of Deuteronomy 2:33: "And the LORD our God delivered him." The second to last letter of Rabin's name, the letter *yod* ׳, appears in the words "sons of Levi." Before the assassination, how could Drosnin or anyone else have known absolutely which of these phrases, if any, related to Rabin's future: "And the LORD our God delivered him," or "will be assassinated," or "sons of Levi"? Logically, at best, Drosnin could only guess which, if any, of these phrases would turn out to be significant.

In his press release criticizing Drosnin's attempts to prophesy future events, Eliyahu Rips, a major Israeli code researcher, presented a text in the Bible where the words "Winston Churchill" are encoded close to the phrase "will be murdered." If Drosnin had found this code years earlier when Churchill was still alive, would he have flown to Britain to warn Winston that his life was in imminent danger? In that case, he would have been mistaken because Winston Churchill died peacefully of natural causes. Therefore, it follows that the placement of Winston Churchill's name near the phrase "will be murdered" was not a code foretelling the future. This illustrates the point that we cannot and should not attempt to use the Bible Codes to predict future events. God forbids fortune-telling and divination of any kind. Significantly, the Israeli researchers, especially Eliyahu Rips, whom Drosnin quotes extensively, have publicly repudiated Drosnin's sensational conclusions that the codes can be used to predict future events such as earthquakes or the next world war. Drosnin has already been proven wrong in his book's false prophecy that there would be a world war in 1996.

As mentioned earlier, the Bible Codes can only be interpreted accurately and confidently after an event has occurred. Then, and only then, can we verify that the codes are legitimate. The Bible Codes support the Bible's claim to be supernatural in its origin. God receives the glory, not the researcher.

Let's examine the real issue. Are the Bible Codes valid? The answer is yes. Do these coded words appear in the biblical text in a manner that is beyond the statistical possibility that this phenomenon is simply a random chance occurrence? Anyone who spends a few hours studying the scholarly articles on the Bible Codes in *Statistical Science* and *Bible Review* will likely conclude that the phenomenon is real. As Dr. David Kazhdan confirmed, this is "serious research carried out by serious investigators."

I have studied the phenomenon of the Bible Codes for the last ten years. In the last six years, I have used computer programs to find new codes and to verify the discoveries of other researchers. I believe that the Bible contains many types of evidence that the Scriptures are inspired by God. The Bible Codes are simply one additional proof that is especially meaningful to our generation in that they could not have been discovered or analyzed until the development of high-speed computers in our lifetime.

It is impossible that any human could have produced so many incredibly complex codes that reveal supernatural knowledge of events that did not occur until thousands of years after the Bible was written. Moreover, the Bible Codes glorify and lift up the name of Jesus Christ. Therefore, I conclude that they are powerful evidence of the inspiration and authority of the Bible. When used in conjunction with the standard apologetic evidence—archeological and historical evidence, advanced scientific and medical statements in the Bible, and evidence from fulfilled prophecy—the Bible Codes will motivate many in our generation to consider the claims of the Bible about Jesus Christ. If we use this material wisely and carefully, in conjunction with these other evidences, we will fulfill God's command to us as revealed in 1 Peter 3:15: "But sanctify the Lord God in your hearts: and be ready always to give an answer to every man that asketh you a reason of the hope that is in you with meekness and fear."

FIVE

New Bible Code Discoveries

Many new codes have been discovered in recent years by various researchers in Israel and North America. In this chapter, I will share many fascinating Bible Codes that provide evidence of the supernatural origin of the Bible as the Word of God.

The Death of Diana, Princess of Wales

Last year millions of people around the world were stunned when the Princess of Wales was killed suddenly in an automobile accident in Paris, France. It was a tragic ending to what began as an almost fairy-tale royal wedding of Lady Diana to Prince Charles, the future king of England. The whole world watched the slow breakup of their marriage and their final separation and divorce. In the final months of Diana's life, she began dating Dodi Fayed, the son of an extremely wealthy Egyptian named Mohammed Fayed, who owns the famous Harrods department store in London. During a visit to Paris in August, 1997, Dodi and Lady Diana were killed in a terrible auto accident when their Mercedes Benz crashed into a concrete pillar in a tunnel that ran beneath a river through the center of the city.

Following the funeral, several members of my staff requested that I run the Bible Codes computer program to search the Bible to see if there might be hidden words in the text referring to this event. Incredibly, virtually every one of the significant words and names of individuals associated with this incident were found encoded in the book of Exodus. Within a small passage surrounding Exodus 28:10, I discovered the following significant words: *princess, Wales, Diana, Spencer* (her family name), *death, river, tunnel, Paris, France, Av* (the month of August), *5757* (the Hebrew year 1997), and *Fayed* פאד, the companion who died in the car with Lady Diana.

Diana, Princess of Wales

Encoded Word	Hebrew	Interval	Reference Begins
Diana	דינה	(49)	Exod. 28:4
Princess	שרי	(29)	Exod. 28:8
Wales	לולם	(62)	Exod. 28:7
Spencer	ספנסר	(29)	Exod. 28:10
Fayed	פאד	(36)	Exod. 28:9
Death	מות	(15)	Exod. 28:8
Paris	פריז	(42)	Exod. 28:15
France	צרפת	(118)	Exod. 27:7
River	נהר	(42)	Exod. 28:8
Tunnel	וקבה	(249)	Exod. 28:4
Av (August)	אב	(14)	Exod. 28:9
5757 (1997)	זנשת	(53)	Exod. 28:12

The Plague of AIDS

Dr. Doron Witztum has discovered a series of encoded words relating to the terrible plague known as Acquired Immune Deficiency Syndrome (AIDS). One of the first passages he found that contains the encoded word "AIDS" appears in Genesis 19:15–17, the passage that describes God's destruction of the wicked cities of Sodom and Gomorrah, the region where homosexuals had unsuccessfully tried to attack the two angels sent by God to warn Lot and his family about the coming destruction.

In another passage in Genesis, the Hebrew word for AIDS is found encoded at 32-letter intervals, from left to right. Also, in Genesis 5:1–8:10, Israeli researchers found a remarkable number of encoded words related to the AIDS virus: *AIDS, in the blood, death, virus, immunity,* and the Hebrew abbreviation for *HIV* (Human Immunodeficiency Virus).

Word	Hebrew	Interval	Reference begins
AIDS	אידס	(-5)	Gen. 5:1
Virus	וירום	(219)	Gen. 6:12
In the blood	בדמ	(-1)	Gen. 5:1
Death	מות	(1)	Gen. 5:1
Immunity	החיסון	(107)	Gen. 8:7
HIV	ההיו	(10)	Gen. 8:10

King Franz Joseph I

Another remarkable Bible Code discovery is the name of King Franz Joseph I, the king of Austria who ruled the Hapsburg royal dynasty from 1848 until his death in 1916.

King Franz Joseph I of the Austrian Empire was quite favorably disposed toward the Jewish people and allowed his Jewish citizens great freedom. In 1869, he made a royal visit to Jerusalem, and the Jewish citizens acclaimed him with great fervor. The great Rabbi Meir Auerbach conferred an unusual public blessing on the king for the favor he had bestowed upon the Jewish people. Dr. Witztum discovered a remarkable cluster of encoded words about this monarch in the portion of Hebrew history that records the Egyptian pharaoh's kindness to Joseph and his family when they came down to Egypt from Canaan to escape the famine. The discovery of the following cluster of Bible Codes—*Franz Joseph, Hapsburg, King of Austria, Jerusalem,* and the name of the rabbi he met, *Auerbach*—provides fascinating evidence regarding the supernatural nature of the Word of God.

Encoded Word	Hebrew	Interval	Reference Begins
Franz	פרנז	(35)	Gen. 45:17
Joseph	יוסף	(1)	Gen. 45:17
Hapsburg	הבסבורג	(-581)	Gen. 44:6
King of Austria	מלך אוסטרי	(9)	Gen. 45:19
Jerusalem	ירושלים	(197)	Gen. 45:11
Auerbach	אוירבכ	(29)	Gen. 45:15

The Peace Process between Israel and the PLO

For the last few years, the eyes of the world have been watching the dangerous peace negotiations between the Palestine Liberation Organization (PLO) and Israel and their desperate search for an elusive peace in the Middle East. Remarkably, a series of encoded words in Deuteronomy, written by Moses over thirty-five hundred years ago, reveals the names of the major participants in these negotiations. In a passage of only thirteen verses, Deuteronomy 8:16–9:8, we find the following encoded words: *Israel; Arafat; PLO; peace treaty;* and the names of both of Israel's former prime ministers who were intensely involved in the peace process, *Yitzchak* (Rabin), and *Shimon Peres.*

Encoded Word	Hebrew	Interval	Reference Begins
Israel	ישראל	(1)	Deut. 9:1
Arafat	ערפאת	(1)	Deut. 9:6
PLO	אשפ	(-15)	Deut. 9:4
Treaty	חוזה	(32)	Deut. 9:7
Peace	שלום	(-14)	Deut. 9:4
Yitzchak	יצחק	(1)	Deut. 9:5
Shimon	שמעון	(92)	Deut. 8:20
Peres	פרס	(-283)	Deut. 8:16

It is noteworthy that these Bible Codes appear in a passage of the Bible that deals with Israel's rebellion against God, when they provoked Him to wrath because they did not trust that He would enable them to possess the whole of the Promised Land. Perhaps significantly, the name of Arafat appears encoded in the surface text in Exodus 33:3 "For thou art a stiff necked people."

Curiously, at the beginning of the peace process, the PLO, an organization outspokenly dedicated to destroying the Jewish people, was at the weakest point in its history, due to dwindling financial support from the Arab nations who had withheld hundreds of millions of dollars in donations because of their anger at the PLO's open support for Saddam Hussein's attack on Kuwait. Consequently, it is hard to understand the decisions of Prime Minister Yitzchak Rabin and Foreign Minister Shimon Peres, as the leaders of Israel, to enter into negotiations to surrender portions of the Promised Land to the PLO. At the time the Madrid peace negotiations began, Prime Minister Rabin decided to surrender the most vital areas of Israel to this fierce enemy at the very moment when the PLO was on its last legs. Even Senator Jesse Helms, the Chairman of the United States Committee on Foreign Relations, was profoundly disturbed by Israel's surrender of land to her deadliest enemies. Senator Helms wrote at the time, "I mistrust Arafat profoundly . . . I will never completely understand how the leaders of Israel reached the decision to enter into negotiations with Yasser Arafat. . . ."[1]

The Assassination of Prime Minister Yitzchak Rabin

The tragic assassination of Prime Minister Yitzchak Rabin stunned the people of Israel and millions of Christians and Jews throughout the world who love the Promised Land and her people. In the days after the assassination, code researchers in Israel and North America naturally scoured the Bible in search of every instance where the name of the late prime minister might be encoded. In an earlier chapter of this book I examined the claim of author Michael Drosnin, who states that he warned the prime minister, based on the occurrence of the coded words "Yitzchak Rabin" in a phrase in Deuteronomy 4:42 that suggested the possibility of assassination.

Another passage of the Torah, however, contains encoded information about Rabin's assassination that is even more extensive. In Genesis 48:13–49:3 we find the encoded names of *Yitzchak Rabin* and *Israel,* the day and year of Rabin's birth, the month and year of his tragic assassination, the name of his assassin, *Yigal Amir,* the phrase *"will be murdered,"* and the word *"Oslo."* Most remarkable is the fact that these eleven Bible Codes are found in just one small passage.

Prime Minister Yitzchak Rabin's Assassination

Encoded Word	Hebrew	Interval	Reference Begins
Yitzchak	יצחק	(1)	Gen. 48:15
Rabin	רבין	(138)	Gen. 48:15
Will be murdered	ירצח	(85)	Gen. 48:13
Yigal	יגאל	(-241)	Gen. 48:16
Amir	עמיר	(15)	Gen. 48:15
Israel	ישראל	(1)	Gen. 48:14
5682 (Year of Rabin's birth)	התרפב	(-225)	Gen. 48:14
1st Adar (Day of Rabin's birth)	אאדר	(-177)	Gen. 48:15
5756 (Year of Rabin's death)	תשנו	(118)	Gen. 48:19
Heshvan (Month of Rabin's death)	חשון	(-285)	Gen. 48:13
Oslo	אוסלו	(182)	Gen. 49:3

Note: The year 5682 in the Hebrew calendar corresponds to 1922, the year Yitzchak Rabin was born. The day of his birth, the first day of Adar, occurred on our March 1. The month of Heshvan in the Hebrew calendar year 5756 corresponds to November 1995.

Bible Codes Relating to the War in the Gulf

Code researchers have also found codes in the book of Genesis that reveal the names of the major participants in the War in the Gulf. During that war, President Saddam Hussein of Iraq attempted to destroy many of the Jews living in Israel by unprovoked missile attacks on Israeli cities. Ten encoded words in the Bible reflect that recent conflict in which God manifested His power to save both the Jews of Israel and the soldiers of America and its allies who fought against the armies of Iraq. Code researchers located the following ten Bible Codes in the book of Genesis: *Saddam* סאראם (President Saddam Hussein of Iraq); *Russian* רוסי and *Scud-B* סקאד בי (the name of the thirty-nine Russian missiles fired against Israel); *the missile will terrify* יבהל טיל (a description of the effect of the Scud-B missiles on those attacked); the *3rd of Shevat* (January 18, 1991, the day of Iraq's first missile attack); *they shut the door* (a phrase that may refer to the sealing of rooms by Israelis to protect against chemical weapons); *George Bush* גורג בוש; *America* אמריקה; *Schwarzkopf* שורצקופ (the general who led the allied armies); and *also in Iraq* והנ בעירק.

The Gulf War Codes

Encoded Word	Hebrew	Interval	Reference Begins
Saddam (Hussein)	סאראם	(6)	Gen. 8:12

And also in Iraq	והנ בעירק	(6)	Gen. 29:9
America	אמריקה	(100)	Gen. 29:2
George Bush	גורג בוש	(-3129)	Gen. 33:8
Schwarzkopf	שורצקופ	(6777)	Gen. 29:24
The missile will terrify	יבהל טיל	(2)	Gen. 19:29
They shut the door	(1) ואת הדלת סגרו		Gen. 19:10
Russian	רוסי	(-1)	Gen. 19:2
Scud-B	סקאד בי	(15)	Gen. 19:1
the 3rd of Shevat	בני בשבט	(-258)	Gen. 20:14

One of the greatest miracles during the War in the Gulf occurred when thirty-nine Russian-designed Scud-B missiles rained down on Tel Aviv, the largest populated area of Israel, where the vast majority of the Jewish state's five million citizens live. Although the American Patriot antimissile system proved of some use in destroying the Scud-B missiles that were launched against United States troops in Saudi Arabia, the same antimissile system did nothing to protect the Jews against these thirty-nine missiles. Several times the Patriot managed to break up incoming Scud-B missiles in the air, but it did not destroy the weapons as hoped. When the missiles landed in Israel, the huge destructive explosives in the warheads of each of these thirty-nine missiles destroyed over fifteen thousand Israeli apartments and homes. The miracle? Not one single Jew was killed by this devastating attack! The odds of this miraculous protection occurring by chance are astronomical. Surely this was a demonstration of the supernatural power of God to preserve His Chosen People from their enemies.

However, another miracle that went almost unreported in the Western news also occurred during those terrifying missile attacks. One of the powerful Scud-B missiles managed to hit its intended target with absolute precision. Although launched from more than five hundred miles away, the Iraqi missile made a direct hit on the Gush Dan main gas-line terminal in Tel Aviv, the line that supplied hundreds of thousands of homes and apartments with gas. The gas lines that extended from that terminal and connected it to every home in the area would normally have been filled with extremely flammable and explosive gas. A missile explosion on a main gas terminal normally would have created a chain reaction of exploding gas below every street in Tel Aviv, creating a fire storm holocaust that would have killed tens of thousands of innocent Israeli citizens.

To the astonishment of the Israeli military, however, there was no secondary explosion when the missile warhead detonated. The fires were immediately extinguished, with no loss of life whatsoever and no chain reaction of exploding gas lines. Just days before the missile attack, technicians working for the utility had detected a minor malfunction in the gas lines that forced the management to shut off and empty the entire gas-line system by draining off all of the gas to allow for a safe inspection and repairs! This miracle reminds me of the tremendous promises of God to protect His people so they can dwell in safety: "But when ye go over Jordan, and dwell in the land which the LORD your God giveth you to inherit, and when he giveth you rest from all your enemies round about, so that ye dwell in safety; then there shall be a place which the LORD your God shall choose to cause his name to dwell there . . ." (Deuteronomy 12:10–11).

In his excellent book, *CompuTorah*,[2] Dr. Moshe Katz has reported that another group of encoded words relating to the War in the Gulf appears in the book of Numbers. The world-wide television network CNN and its star reporter Peter Arnet were watched virtually every day of the conflict by millions around the world. In the book of Numbers, researchers in Israel found the encoded names of CNN and Peter Arnet. In fact, Peter Arnet's full name appears in code in one single verse, Numbers 36:5. His first name "Peter" פיטר is encoded left to right at 4-letter intervals, and his last name "Arnet" ארנט is encoded right to left at 2-letter intervals.

War in the Gulf: The CNN Codes

Encoded Word	Hebrew	Interval	Reference Begins
CNN	סי-אנ-אנ	(-780)	Num. 33:28
Peter	פיטר	(-4)	Num. 36:5
Arnet	ארנט	(2)	Num. 36:5

The Oklahoma City Bombing

On April 19, 1995, the worst terrorist attack in the history of North America destroyed the United States Murrah Building and killed 169 innocent people. For the first time, the heartland of America became vulnerable to the terrorism and madness that has afflicted so many other countries of the world during the last few decades. This tragic event destroyed forever the feeling of security that had been known by generations of Americans who felt they were immune from the random terrorist violence experienced by other nations throughout the modern world.

The trial of the accused bomber concluded with the conviction and death sentence of Timothy McVeigh, who was found guilty by a jury for intentionally killing the innocent civilians who happened to work in the federal government building. The evidence put forward at the trial suggested that Timothy McVeigh was motivated by an intense hatred of the United States government. Apparently, this hatred had festered in McVeigh from the time of the government's disastrous military-style attack, two years earlier, on the Branch Davidians, a strange messianic cult living near Waco, Texas. The fiery debacle at the Branch Davidian compound led to the tragic death of many innocent lives, children included. It was the worst massacre of civilians in United States history.

According to testimony given at his trial, McVeigh apparently decided to exact his revenge against the government on the second anniversary of the April 19, 1993, destruction of the Branch Davidian compound by the FBI and United States military support units. Tragically, McVeigh was successful in destroying the Murrah Building and hundreds of citizens. Serious questions remain unanswered as to the possible foreknowledge of this terrorist event by agencies of the United States government who may have infiltrated McVeigh's group but somehow failed to stop the attack in time to avert disaster. This event remains the single most destructive terrorist attack to date in the history of North America.

Ten specific Bible Codes have been found in the Bible that describe detailed aspects of the tragedy that occurred on April 19, 1995, in Oklahoma City. The following codes, discovered in the book of Genesis, appear to relate to the Oklahoma bombing: Oklahoma אוקלהומה; terror חתת;

Murrah מורה; *Building* ביריג; *desolated, slaughtered* שממזבח; *death* מות; *his name is Timothy* שמו טימותי; *McVeigh* מקוויי; *day 19* יומיט; *on the 9th hour* שעהט; *in the morning* בבקר. This incredible list of Bible Codes describes a tragic event in history that will affect the world for many years. The list below includes information about where these ten encoded words are found in the Hebrew Bible. Anyone with a Hebrew-English Interlinear Bible or the Bible Codes software program will be able to verify these Bible Codes.

The Oklahoma City Bombing

Encoded Word	Hebrew	Interval	Reference Begins
Oklahoma	אוקלהומה	(-1445)	Gen. 35:5
Terror	חתת	(1)	Gen. 35:5
Murrah	מורה	(-5)	Gen. 36:8
Building	ביריג	(96)	Gen. 36:24
Desolated, slaughtered	שממזבח	(1)	Gen. 35:7
Death	מות	(19)	Gen. 35:7
His name is Timothy	שמו טימותי	(-377)	Gen. 44:4
McVeigh	מקוויי	(389)	Gen. 34:21
Day 19	יומיט	(191)	Gen. 32:13
On the 9th hour	שעהט	(-126)	Gen. 34:18
In the morning	בבקר	(47)	Gen. 36:10

The Terrorist Assassination of
Israeli Policeman Nissim Toledano

One of the most extraordinary groups of Bible Codes relates to a relatively little-known event that occurred in Israel in the winter of 1992, involving the terrorist assassination of an Israeli border policeman, First Sergeant Nissim Toledano. He was assassinated by Arab terrorists from Hamas, an Islamic organization that refuses to accept the existence of the state of Israel. The leadership of Hamas sent a three-man team of Palestinian Arabs into Israel with the goal of assassinating an Israeli soldier or police officer. Three Arab terrorists infiltrated into Israel, stole a car, and searched for a target of opportunity. As the three-man terrorist team approached the Ben Guerion airport outside the city of Lod, they drove by an Israeli border policeman, First Sergeant Toledano, who was waiting for a bus.

The terrorists decided to kill their innocent target, First Sergeant Toledano, with their stolen car—a hit and run. However, after hitting him, they looked back and noticed he was still moving. They backed up the car, pulled their victim into the car, and sped away. Some Israelis who were approaching the bus stop saw the kidnapping and alerted the authorities. After the reports of the kidnapping became public knowledge on the Israeli radio network that night, the whole nation realized the extreme threat to the Jewish population from random terrorist attacks.

Dr. Moshe Katz, one of the most brilliant of the Israeli Bible Code researchers who has examined the code phenomenon for a decade, conducted a Bible Code search for the name of the kidnapped victim. Dr. Katz found the name of the victim, *Toledano*, together with the words *captivity, Lod, first sergeant,* and *border police.* His incredible code discovery is described in his book, *CompuTorah.*

The Captivity of Toledano

Encoded Word	Hebrew	Interval	Reference Begins
The captivity of Toledano	לשביית טולינו	(3191)	Gen. 21:23
First sergeant	רב סמל	(5)	Gen. 48:8
Border police	מג"ב	(2)	Gen. 31:39
Lod	לוד	(-1)	Gen. 39:14

Immediately after the kidnapping, the terrorists had an argument in the car regarding what they should do with their captive. One terrorist argued for his immediate murder with a dagger, while his two companions suggested that Toledano be kept alive to be used as a ransom in exchange for their imprisoned terrorist comrades. Finally, the three terrorists decided to kill Toledano, but they disagreed as to whether they should kill him with a knife or smother him. One terrorist suggested that they should "shed no blood." Another suggested that they smother him to death. Finally, after failing in their attempt to smother Toledano, one terrorist said, "Let's kill him." They used a knife to kill the policeman, and they cast his body into a pit in the desert. Three days later, the body of Toledano was found in a pit, and the Israeli security forces succeeded in capturing the three terrorists. In response to this terrible act, the Israeli government exiled four hundred notorious Hamas terrorists to the northern

Lebanese border, most of whom had previously been con-victed of various terrorist crimes against Israeli citizens. Naturally, the United Nations condemned Israel's mild actions against her worst and most deadly enemies.

Following the Israeli security forces' arrest of the three ter-rorists, the captured men recounted to the police their assas-sination plans and the argument they had in the car about how to kill their victim. Incredibly, the reported conversa-tions of these murderers corresponded to information revealed in the encoded words discovered by Dr. Katz. When the names of these members of the Hamas terrorist team were published in several Israeli newspapers, Dr. Katz went back to his computer and input their names: Atun, Abu Katish, and Isa. To his amazement, all three names were found encoded at minimal ELS intervals in the book of Genesis.

The Names of the Three Terrorists
Who Killed Toledano

Encoded Name	Hebrew	Interval	Reference Begins
Atun	עטרן	(19)	Gen. 41:45
Abu Katish	אבו קתיש	(-1584)	Gen. 37:22
Isa	עיסא	(2)	Gen. 41:16

In his search for the Toledano codes, all of which he found clustered in the book of Genesis, Dr. Katz made another dis-covery. With the newspaper accounts of the terrorists' con-fession in hand, he realized that there was a remarkable similarity between the events of the kidnapping and murder of Toledano and the Genesis account of Joseph, who was thrown into a deep pit in the desert and left for dead by his jealous brothers. In this Genesis account, we find that the same phrases that were uttered by Joseph's brothers thousands of years ago were also uttered by the three terrorists:

"let's kill him" (Genesis 37:21)
"shed no blood" (Genesis 37:22)
"cast him" (Genesis 37:22)
"in the desert" (Genesis 37:22)
"lay no hand upon him" (Genesis 37:22)
"cried in a loud voice" (Genesis 39:14)
"he will die" (Genesis 44:31)

The discovery of the precise details of the death of Nissim Toledano encoded in the text of Genesis is very thought provoking. If the history of this private man is encoded, is it possible that the Bible Codes may contain information about an overwhelming number of other topics? It is important to remember that this research of the Bible Codes has only begun in the last few years. Much more remains to be discovered.

The Hebron Massacre

One of the saddest events in the history of modern Israel occurred when an American-born Jewish doctor, Baruch Goldstein, mercilessly attacked a group of Moslem worshipers who were peaceably worshipping in the ancient Cave of the Patriarchs in Hebron. This ancient building was built by Herod the Great two thousand years ago to surround the cave that contained the revered tombs of Abraham, Sarah, and other patriarchs who are honored ancestors to Muslims, Christians, and Jews. This site, on which sits both a synagogue and a mosque, is sacred to Jews and Muslims alike. Both groups accept the ancient tradition that the site is the ancient burial place of the patriarchs of both the Israeli Jews and the Arab Muslims.

Dr. Goldstein was descended from a Jewish family who had experienced the brutal 1929 Arab massacre and riot that killed most of the Jews living in Hebron during the years of the British Mandate. Dr. Goldstein had moved to the city of Hebron to assist the Jewish settlers in rebuilding one of the most sacred of the ancient cities of the Promised Land.

However, as a doctor, Goldstein was constantly dealing with the bloody results of Arab PLO terrorism against both innocent Jews and Palestinians. Few Western readers realize that the Arab terrorists are relatively indifferent to the suffering caused to their Arab brethren by their terrorist attacks on the Jews because they believe that the innocent Muslim victims of their attacks will go to heaven as honored martyrs of the Palestinian cause. When one of his close friends was killed by terrorists, Dr. Goldstein became almost insane with grief and anger. He took an army assault rifle and attacked a group of Muslim worshipers, killing and wounding thirty-nine of them in a mad act of revenge. The encoded words below appear to relate to this tragic event. Significantly, the last letter in the encoded word *Goldstein* forms the first letter of the word *revenge*.

The Hebron Massacre

Encoded Word	Hebrew	Interval	Reference Begins
Cave of the Patriarchs	מערת המכפלה	(1)	Gen. 25:9

82

Baruch	ברון	(-1)	Exod. 13:15
Goldstein	גלדרשטין	(9193)	Exod. 31:10
Revenge	נקמה	(-1)	Lev. 25:16
Year 5689			
(1929)	ה"תרפט	(18)	Lev. 19:21
Al Fatah			
(Arafat's PLO)	חת-פלא	(1)	Lev. 19:21

The Name of God Encoded in the Book of Esther

It has always been a mystery to Jews and Christians why the book of Esther is the only book in the Bible in which the name God does not appear. Because of this omission of the word *God,* some theologians have suggested that Esther should not have been included in the canon of Holy Scripture. However, by using computer analysis, we can demonstrate that the word *Lord* הוהי appears in this small book of Esther three times at small ELS intervals of 3, -37, and -31. For example, in Esther 7:7 the word *Lord* הוהי is encoded at a 3-letter interval.

Hidden Bible Codes Found in the Relevant Biblical Passages

Numerous researchers have discovered that encoded names of biblical personalities appear in the Scriptures precisely in the verse where the biblical text is speaking of the named individual. The odds of this occurring by random chance are astronomical. For example, the name *Abel* הבל is encoded at 49-letter intervals in Genesis 4:23–25, a passage that discusses avenging in relation to the killing of Abel by his brother Cain. In addition, the name *Cain* קין is also located at 49-letter intervals in Genesis 4:13–15.

Another interesting example of a significantly located ELS code is the word *Babel* בבל encoded every 49 letters in Genesis 11:1–3, a passage that describes the building of the tower of Babel in ancient Babylon.

Codes Reveal Rabbi Maimonides and His Book *Mishneh Torah*

Of the early code discoveries, one of the most interesting was made by Rabbi Weissmandl. He found the beloved name of the greatest Jewish rabbi, Moses ben Maimonides (died A.D. 1204). Maimonides was affectionately known as "Rambam," a name derived from the Hebrew letters that make up his name (Robot Moftai Beretz Mitzraim = RMBM). This name is found encoded at a 4-letter interval from right to left in a phrase in Exodus 11:9, which reads, "that my wonders may be multiplied in the land of Egypt."

As a doctor for the royal Muslim court in Egypt, Rambam was famous for his near miraculous medical cures. Amazingly, the word *Mishneh* משנה, the first word in the title of Maimonides' most famous book, *Mishneh Torah*, is also encoded in Exodus 11:9 at 50-letter intervals, and the word *Torah* תורה, the second word in the title of his book, is encoded in Exodus 12:11, also at 50-letter intervals. Moreover, the two encoded words are located precisely 613 letters apart in the Hebrew text of the Torah. This is remarkable in light of the fact that both the Torah and Maimonides' lifelong study, *Mishneh Torah,* deal specifically with the 613 commandments and laws of God found in the Bible. In fact, according to a mathematical analysis by Dr. Daniel

Michelson of the Department of Mathematics at UCLA in his review "Reading the Torah with Equal Intervals," the odds of these two meaningful and related words, *Mishneh* משנה and *Torah* תורה, occurring precisely 613 letters apart by random chance are 1 chance in 186 million.

Twenty-Five Trees Encoded in Genesis 2

In my book *The Signature of God,* I reported the discovery by the Israeli code researchers of the encoded names of twenty-five trees in Genesis 2, the chapter about God's creation of Adam and Eve and the plants and animals in the Garden of Eden.[3] Each one of the twenty-five trees mentioned by name in the rest of the Old Testament appears encoded in this short chapter (635 words in English). There is no other passage in the Old Testament that contains the encoded names of these twenty-five trees at intervals of less than 20 letters. In addition, the researchers found the name "Eden" encoded sixteen times in this same passage.

The Names of Twenty-Five Trees
Encoded in Genesis 2

Encoded Name	Hebrew
Vine	גפן
Grape	ענב
Chestnut	ערמן
Dense forest	עבת
Date	תמר
Acacia	שטה

Bramble	אטד
Cedar	ארז
Nut	בטן
Fig	תאנה
Willow	ערבה
Pomegranate	רמון
Aloe	אהלים
Tamarisk	אשל
Oak	אלון
Poplar	לבנה
Cassia	קדה
Almond	שקד
Mastic	אלה
Thorn bush	סנה
Hazel	לוז
Olive	זית
Citron	הדר
Fir	גפר
Wheat (possibly tree of knowledge)	חטה

Obviously, the encoding of the Hebrew names of these trees
is not prophetic. However, it would be very complicated, to
say the least, for anyone to attempt to write a meaningful
short story about any topic while, at the same time, encoding
twenty-five names of trees at ELS intervals within the text.
Over the last eighteen months since the publication of *The
Signature of God,* I have stated in various meetings and radio
programs that I believe someone could purposely encode ELS
words such as the twenty-five trees, but it would be very difficult. To make my point I offered a challenge of $1000 to the
first person to demonstrate to me in writing that he or she has

purposely encoded twenty-five names of trees within an English text of similar length as Genesis 2 without using a computer program. In January 1998, eighteen months after I first offered the challenge, Gidon Cohen, from the United Kingdom, became the first person to successfully complete my challenge and collected the $1000 prize (please don't send me any other attempts).

Nevertheless, the ELS codes found in Genesis 2 are far more complicated than the specifications of my public challenge. In my own recent computer Bible Code research on this fascinating portion of Genesis 2, I found that God had also encoded many other Bible Codes within this same passage, in particular, the names of seventeen animals that appear in the Old Testament. Furthermore, the name *Torah* is also encoded five times, and the name *Yeshua* is found ten times in this same passage. These incredibly complex codes appear embedded within a pattern of "wheels within wheels" in a text that flows quite naturally. In other words, there appears to be nothing artificial or contrived in the choice of words that the author has used to express the story of God's creation of mankind in the Garden of Eden.

A brilliant new code search program has just been developed in Isreal that enables English speakers to search personally for Bible codes throughout the Old Testament without having to know Hebrew. An evaluation of the new *Bible Codes Plus* software can be examined at the following internet site: http://www.grantjeffrey.com.

Among the most fascinating code discoveries made in recent years is the discovery that God has encoded the names of Jesus and His disciples, and numerous other individuals involved in Jesus' life and ministry, in two different portions of the Old Testament. In the following chapters that deal with the Yeshua codes and the Messiah codes, you will find overwhelming evidence that these codes describe virtually every significant person in the life of Christ. However, they were hidden in the text of the Old Testament, written seven centuries before Jesus of Nazareth was born. In addition, we will examine code discoveries about Jesus Christ that will provide powerful evidence of the supernatural origin of the Scriptures and the identification of Jesus as the true Messiah.

SIX

The Yeshua Codes

The Name of Jesus Encoded in the Old Testament

Of all the code discoveries I have researched and shared with my readers, none thrill me more than the Yeshua codes. God has actually hidden the name *Yeshua* (the Hebrew name of Jesus) throughout the Old Testament in significant passages from Genesis to Malachi, beginning with the first word of the first verse in Genesis: "In the beginning God created the heaven and the earth" (Genesis 1:1). Starting with the fifth letter (*yod* י) in the first word, *Bereishis* בראשית "In the beginning," and counting forward every 521st letter, the phrase *Yeshua yakhol,* "Jesus is able," is spelled out.

I came across the discovery of the Yeshua codes quite providentially. Once I had fully appreciated that the Bible Codes reveal a large amount of information about historical events, I naturally wondered if God had secretly encoded the Hebrew name of Jesus Christ in the text of the Old Testament. Providentially, several years ago I received a request from Yacov Rambsel, asking if he could quote from research material on the laws of probability with respect to the fulfillment of messianic prophecies in the life, death, and resurrection of Jesus that I had used in my book *Armageddon: Appointment with Destiny*. Rambsel has ministered as a pastor and leader of a messianic congregation of believers in San Antonio, Texas. He has been independently researching the Hebrew Scriptures for the last eight years in his study of the Bible Codes about Yeshua. What is remarkable is the fact that Rambsel does his research manually, without a computer.

In discussing this material with Rambsel, I realized that he had a real passion for the study of the Scriptures and for Jesus Christ as his Messiah. After I completed my chapter "Mysterious Bible Codes" in my book *The Signature of God* in April 1996, I asked Rambsel to review the Hebrew text for accuracy because he had spent years studying the Hebrew Scriptures.

Rambsel told me that he had just completed his own book on the Bible Codes that focused on a series of extraordinary discoveries that he had made independently. Rambsel's research provided the answer to my question about whether God had encoded the name of Jesus within the Hebrew Scriptures. With Rambsel's permission, I will share a small portion of the phenomenal research that he has completed during thousands of hours of painstaking analysis of the hidden ELS codes. I highly recommend Yacov Rambsel's two books to anyone who is fascinated by this research: *YESHUA: The Name of Jesus Revealed in the Old Testament*[1] and its sequel, *His Name Is Jesus*.[2]

Most Bible Code researchers use complex computer programs to search for Bible Codes. For example, I have three software programs that I purchased in Jerusalem during the 1991 War in the Gulf. Rambsel, however, does all his detailed analysis manually. He patiently examines the text of the Old Testament and manually counts the equally spaced intervals between letters. The work and dedication involved to do this kind of manual analysis of the Bible is staggering.

There are many detailed prophecies about Jesus Christ in the Old Testament. One of the most astonishing discoveries Rambsel has made is that the name Yeshua is encoded in virtually every one of the major Old Testament prophecies about the coming of the Messiah Jesus. One of the most significant of the Yeshua codes, "Yeshua is My name" שמי ישוע, is found in the important messianic prophecy of Isaiah 53:8–10, the passage that prophesies the trial, death, and crucifixion of Jesus Christ. Verse 10, in particular, depicts the atoning sacrifice that Christ made for our sins when He offered Himself as the Lamb of God—a perfect sacrifice—on the cross two thousand years ago: "Yet it pleased the LORD to bruise him; he hath put him to grief: when thou shalt make his soul an offering for sin, he shall see his seed, he shall prolong his days, and the pleasure of the LORD shall prosper in his hand" (Isaiah 53:10).

Beginning with the second Hebrew letter, *yod* ‏ י, in the phrase "He shall prolong" *ya'arik* יאריך, Rambsel counted forward every 20th letter from right to left and discovered the phrase ישוע שמי *Yeshua Shmi,* which means "Yeshua [Jesus] is My name." This same passage in Isaiah actually contains a unique series of Bible Codes that will be discussed in the next chapter.

A passage in the Book of Genesis declares that the Lord provided "coats of skin" for Adam and Eve to cover their nakedness after they sinned: "And Adam called his wife's name Eve; because she was the mother of all living. Unto Adam also and to his wife did the Lord God make coats of skins, and clothed them" (Genesis 3:20–21). This significant verse reveals that God killed the first animal in history as a sacrifice for sin and for a covering for the nakedness of Adam and Eve. This provision symbolized the Passover lamb that God later commanded the Israelites to sacrifice every Passover to commemorate their salvation in the Exodus from Egypt. However, this act also symbolized the future perfect sacrifice of the Lamb of God to atone for the sins of all those who will confess and ask Christ to forgive them. This important passage also contains an encoded phrase about Jesus as the true Lamb of God. Beginning with the last *heh* ה in Genesis 3:20 and counting forward every 9th letter, we find the word *Yoshiah*, meaning "He will save."

The word *Yoshiah* (Joshua) is a Hebrew equivalent name for *Yeshua* (Jesus). This encoded name *Yoshiah*, meaning "He will save," reminds us of the parallel message given to the young virgin Mary by the angel who declared "thou shalt call his name Jesus: for he shall save his people from their sins" (Matthew 1:21). The same passage in Genesis (3:20–21) also contains another Bible Code that refers to Jesus.

The Betrayal of Yeshua by Judas Iscariot

Of all the messianic codes Rambsel has found, the passage that predicts the betrayal of Jesus by His disciple Judas Iscariot is one of the most startling: "A thing of ruin is poured out on Him; and He Who lies down shall not rise again. Even My own familiar friend, in whom I trusted, who did eat of My bread, has lifted up his heel against Me."

(Psalm 41:8–9). Rambsel found that beginning in verse 8 with the letter *yod* י, in the phrase "they plot evil" *yach'shvu rah'ah,* and counting forward every 2nd letter from right to left spells *Yeshua* ישוע. This ELS code continues to spell out the word *chavrah,* which indicates that Judas was part of a group. In other words, in the exact verse in which King David predicted the tragic betrayal of Jesus the Messiah over one thousand years before it occurred, we also find the name of the person betrayed—*Yeshua*—encoded at 2-letter intervals. The statistical study "Statistical Significance Discovered in the Yeshua Codes," by Guy Cramer and Lori Eldridge (published on the Internet[3]), suggests that the odds are only 1 chance in 26,790 that this phrase, *Yeshua chavrah*, occurs by random chance in this prophecy.

One of the most well-known messianic prophecies in the Old Testament describes the exact price of Christ's betrayal, thirty pieces of silver. Over five hundred years before the birth of Jesus, the prophet Zechariah wrote this prediction: "And I said unto them, If ye think good, give me my price; and if not, forbear. So they weighed for my price thirty pieces of silver" (Zechariah 11:12). Beginning with the letter *yod* י in the phrase "my price" *se'kari* and counting forward every 24th letter spells the name *Yeshua* ישוע. In this prophecy describing the exact price of our Lord's betrayal, written five hundred years before Christ's birth, God included an encoded message to His Chosen People that identified the name of the promised Messiah—*Yeshua* Jesus.

In the verses that follow this prediction of Christ's first coming, the prophet Zechariah looks forward twenty-five centuries into the future to describe the incredible emotional upheaval and mourning that will occur when the spiritual eyes of the Jewish people are opened to see that the Messiah whom they rejected for twenty centuries is, in fact, their Messiah Yeshua, the Son of God. Zechariah prophetically saw Jesus' second coming to save Israel from the Antichrist's armies, following the battle of Armageddon. Then the Jews will see Jesus as their true Messiah: "And I will pour upon the house of David, and upon the inhabitants of Jerusalem, the spirit of grace and of supplications: and they shall look upon me whom they have pierced, and they shall mourn for him, as one mourneth for his only son, and shall be in bitterness for him, as one that is in bitterness for his firstborn" (Zechariah 12:10). Beginning with the letter *chet* ח in the phrase "an only son" *ha'yachid* and counting forward every 38th letter, Rambsel discovered the word *Mashiach* משיח "Messiah."

Yeshua, the Great High Priest

We are taught throughout the Scriptures that Jesus Christ is our great High Priest: "But Christ being come an high priest of good things to come, by a greater and more perfect tabernacle, not made with hands, that is to say, not of this building" (Hebrews 9:11). In Leviticus, Moses revealed God's detailed instructions regarding the rules for the anointing of the holy priesthood and the sacrifices for the sins of the Chosen People. "And he that is the high priest among his brethren, upon whose head the anointing oil was poured, and that is consecrated to put on the garments, shall not uncover his head, nor rend his clothes; Neither shall he go in to any dead body, nor defile himself for his father, or for his mother; Neither shall he go out of the sanctuary, nor profane the sanctuary of his God; for the crown of the anointing oil of his God is upon him: I am the Lᴏʀᴅ" (Leviticus 21:10–12). This passage about the anointing of the high priest, which contains a code about the blood of Jesus Christ shed for our sins, prophetically speaks to us of the great High Priest, Jesus the Messiah, who gave Himself, once and for all, as a sacrifice for our sins through His sacrificial death on the cross.

The anointing of the high priest of Israel prophetically prefigures the anointing of Jesus at His second coming, which will be accomplished with the anointing oil (recently found hidden near Qumran by the Dead Sea) described in Exodus 30:25–35. Rambsel examined this passage and found that beginning with the first *heh* ה in Leviticus 21:10 and counting forward every 3rd letter spells the phrase *hain dam Yeshua,* which means "Behold! The blood of Yeshua."

The study "Statistical Significance Discovered in the Yeshua Codes" was published on the Internet in 1997. This study calculated the probability that this phrase "Behold! The blood of Yeshua," could appear encoded by random chance at a 3-letter interval in a book the size of Leviticus. Its conclusion is that the odds against this happening are so great that you would have to search through 69,711 books the size of Leviticus to discover this phrase at a 3-letter interval.

Another key prophetic passage, Psalm 72:13–15, contains the Bible Code *Yeshua* ישרע, encoded at 19-letter intervals in the phrase "shall save the souls of the needy. He shall redeem their soul. . . ." The Bible Code in this passage reveals that *Yeshua* ישרע is Jesus, the source of our personal salvation from sin and guilt.

More than seven centuries before the birth of Jesus, Isaiah the prophet announced that Jesus would come as the great liberator of mankind. Isaiah's prophecy of the great jubilee at the end of this age reminded Israel that their

Messiah would finally cancel all their debts and proclaim liberty to all those who were captives to sin. "The Spirit of the Lord GOD is upon me; because the LORD hath anointed me to preach good tidings unto the meek; he hath sent me to bind up the brokenhearted, to proclaim liberty to the captives, and the opening of the prison to those who are bound; to proclaim the acceptable year of the LORD, and the day of vengeance of our God; to comfort all that mourn" (Isaiah 61:1–2). Starting with the *yod* ׳ in the phrase "The Spirit of the Lord GOD" *Ruach Adonai Elohim* and counting every 9 letters from left to right spells *Yeshua*. In addition, Rambsel discovered that the word *Oshiyah* אׄוׄשׄיׄעׄ is also encoded, beginning with the last letter *aleph* א in the second verse and counting every 36th letter from left to right. The word *Oshiyah*, meaning "I will save," is a variation of the word *Yeshua* Jesus.

Yeshua Revealed in Daniel's Vision of the Seventy Weeks

Of the many discoveries made by Yacov Rambsel, one of the most significant concerns the great prophecy of Daniel's Vision of the Seventy Weeks in Daniel 9:25–27: "Know therefore and understand, that from the going forth of the commandment to restore and to build Jerusalem unto the Messiah the Prince shall be seven weeks, and threescore and two weeks: the street shall be built again, and the wall, even in troublous times. And after threescore and two weeks shall Messiah be cut off, but not for himself: and the people of the prince that shall come shall destroy the city and the sanctuary; and the end thereof shall be with a flood, and unto the end of the war desolations are determined. And he shall confirm the covenant with many for one week: and in the midst of the week he shall cause the sacrifice and the oblation to cease, and for the overspreading of abominations he shall make it desolate, even until the consummation, and that determined shall be poured upon the desolate."

Students of the Bible are familiar with the controversy over the last century about the correct identity of the "Messiah the Prince" in verse 25. Those who deny that the prophecy refers to Jesus Christ's first coming usually claim that "Messiah the Prince" actually refers to King Hezekiah or some other historical person. However, Rambsel made a wonderful discovery. He found the name *Yeshua* ישרע in Daniel 9:26, starting with the letter *yod* י in the phrase "the city" *v'ha'iry* and counting every 26th letter from left to right. In addition, in Daniel's prophecy of the Seventy Weeks, Rambsel found the name *Nazarene* נצרי encoded at 112-letter intervals, together with the following encoded words: *King* מלכ (46), *Branch* נצר (50), *Jesse* ישי (10), and *Messiah* משׁיח (52).

Encoded Word	Hebrew	Interval	Reference Begins
Yeshua	ישׁרע	(-26)	Dan. 9:26
Nazarene	נצרי	(112)	Dan. 9:23
King	מלך	(46)	Dan. 9:24
Branch	נצר	(50)	Dan. 9:24
Jesse	ישי	(10)	Dan. 9:25
Messiah	משׁיח	(52)	Dan. 9:25

Psalm 22: The Prophecy of the Crucified Messiah

A thousand years before Jesus of Nazareth was born, King

David wrote the prophetic Psalm 22, which predicts the death of Jesus by crucifixion: "They pierced my hands and my feet." Execution by crucifixion had not even been invented when King David made his remarkable prediction. In addition, David's prophecy also reveals that the soldiers would gamble for the garments of Christ: "For dogs have compassed me: the assembly of the wicked have enclosed me: they pierced my hands and my feet. I may tell all my bones: they look and stare upon me. They part my garments among them, and cast lots upon my vesture" (Psalm 22:16–18). The clear fulfillment of David's prophetic psalm in the life and death of Jesus of Nazareth on the cross is confirmed by a group of Bible Codes found clustered at low intervals in this important prophetic passage about the crucified Messiah.

The word *Yeshua* ישוע is found encoded from right to left within the larger Hebrew word מישועתי, which means "from salvation of me." In addition, this prophetic passage contains other significant Bible Codes that reveal a great deal of information about the future Messiah of Israel, Yeshua: He would be the *anointed* one, raised in *Nazareth*, descended from *Jesse*, and declared *King of the Jews*. He was named *Yeshua* by the angel who appeared to Mary because "He will *save* His people from their sins." Jesus also fulfilled the prophecies of the *Branch* found in the book of Zechariah.

Psalm 22: The Crucified Messiah

Encoded Word	Hebrew	Interval	Reference Begins
Yeshua	ישוע	(1)	Ps. 22:2
Anoint	משח	(6)	Ps. 22:9

King	מלך	(8)	Ps. 22:10
Branch	נצר	(3)	Ps. 22:11
Jesse	ישי	(14)	Ps. 22:12
Messiah	משיח	(8)	Ps. 22:14
Nazareth	נצרי	(-7)	Ps. 22:19
Salvation	ישע	(49)	Ps. 22:24

Is the Original Hebrew Name of Jesus
Yeshua ישע or *Yeshu* ישו?

Some Yeshua code critics have claimed that the name *Yeshua* ישע is not the name that Jesus of Nazareth used during His lifetime. They claim that *Yeshu* ישו—a name Jews often use today to refer to Jesus—is the correct name. The Israeli critics of the Yeshua codes have suggested on the Internet that "Yeshua is a recent, manipulative invention used to facilitate the proselytization of Jews."

The Hebrew name used by first-century Jews to refer to Jesus is of obvious importance to Christians and Jews alike. In Palestine, in the first half of this century, the linguist Eliezer Ben-Yehuda recreated the ancient Hebrew language as a basis for a common language for the nation of Israel. He began with the ancient Hebrew words used in the Bible and in Temple worship and then expanded the vocabulary with new, modern words based on biblical Hebrew forms and rules of grammar. In the prolegomenon to his thesaurus of the Hebrew language, *Thesaurus Totius Hebraitatis,* he discusses the name of Jesus. According to a study on this subject by Professor Kai Kjoer-Hansen in the magazine *Mishkan,* Ben-Yehuda refers to Jesus, using the spelling *Yeshua,* eight times. Although the name *Yeshu* is used most often today in Israel, historical evidence strongly supports the claim that the original Hebrew name of Jesus was *Yeshua* ישרע.

How did the name *Yeshua* ישרע become transformed to the shortened form *Yeshu* ישו? The answer is not simple. As the Church expanded throughout the Roman Empire in the first century, Jewish and rabbinic opposition to Jesus grew. The modified spelling of the name Jesus (*Yeshu* ישו) began to appear in the rabbinic literature that rejected the Christian claims about Jesus of Nazareth. Some ancient sources suggest that shortening a name was a derogatory means to refer to someone you had rejected. There is a type of ancient Jewish literature called *Toledoth Yeshu* that was anti-Jesus. This literature reveals that some Jews purposely changed the name of *Yeshua* ישרע to *Yeshu* ישו to reflect their rejection of His claims to be their Messiah and the Son of God. The ancient Jewish enemies of Jesus used the expression *Yimach Shemo Uzikhro* "May his name and memory be blotted out" as a curse. The first letter of each word of the curse formed the three-letter acronym ישו—the same spelling as *Yeshu*. However, today most modern Jews who commonly use the name *Yeshu* ישו have no knowledge of this possible reason why Jews have historically chosen to call Jesus by that name.

The great Jewish rabbi Moses Maimonides, known as "Rambam" (A.D. 1204), wrote about Jesus in his *Epistle to Yemen* and in *Mishneh Torah,* his monumental fourteen-volume study that codified all of the religious laws from the Torah. In both of these works, he used the name *Yeshua* ישרע to refer to Jesus.

I acquired the uncensored edition of Rambam's *Mishneh Torah* in a Jewish bookstore in Jerusalem several years ago. Most editions in the last eight hundred years were censored, and the passages referring to Jesus of Nazareth were removed. However, when the Jews of Yemen flew back to Israel in the 1950s, they carried with them uncensored original copies of Maimonides' great work that dated back to the twelveth century. Rabbi Eliyahu Touger translated and edited this particular volume, which was published by the Maznaim Publishing Corporation in New York and Jerusalem in 1987. In his edition, Rabbi Touger wrote the following in a footnote: "Though most published texts of the *Mishneh Torah* conclude this chapter with this paragraph, a large portion of the Rambam's text was censored and left unpublished. We have included the original text, based on the Yemenite manuscripts of *Mishneh Torah* and early uncensored editions."[4]

In *The Laws of Kings and Their Wars,* a book about the qualifications of the true Messiah, Rabbi Maimonides referred to Jesus of Nazareth twice, again spelling His name ישוע *Yeshua.* Quoting from this work, "Jesus of Nazareth who aspired to be the Messiah and was executed by the court was also [alluded to] in Daniel's prophecies. . . ."[5] The Hebrew words "Jesus of Nazareth" are spelled in Hebrew as follows: ישוע הנוצרי.

The name Yeshua is related to the name of Joshua, the son of Nun. His name was spelled Yehoshua. The form Yeshua is a short form of the longer name Yehoshua, as demonstrated in Nehemiah 8:17, where the biblical writer refers to Joshua using the shortened form Yeshua: "And all the congregation of them that were come again out of the captivity made booths, and sat under the booths: for since the days of Jeshua [ישוע] the son of Nun unto that day had not the children of Israel done so. And there was very great gladness" (Nehemiah 8:17). Ezra also refers to a man by the name of "Jozabad the son of Jeshua" using the same spelling, *Yeshua* ישוע.

In addition to the clear biblical evidence that the name *Yeshua* ישרע was used in biblical times, there is archeological evidence as well. Archeologists found the name *Yeshua* ישרע in various texts of the Dead Sea Scrolls found at Qumran, including a scroll known as 4QT Testimonium. They have also discovered ossuaries (stone coffins) in a first-century burial cave near Bethany. Coins found in the ossuaries that were minted by Herod Agrippa (A.D. 42) confirm the period of burial. The lids or sides of these ossuaries were inscribed with the names of the Jewish Christians who were buried within. A number of the ossuaries were inscribed with the sign of the cross and with the name *Yeshua,* some in Hebrew and others in Greek. This find, reported by French archeologist M. Clermont-Ganneau, was published in the Palestine Exploration Fund Quarterly Statement, January 1874. In 1931 the archeologist E. L. Sukenik also described the discovery of a first-century ossuary with the name *Yeshua* ישרע.

In light of the overwhelming evidence presented in this chapter, I believe we can have confidence that the name *Yeshua* ישרע is the genuine Hebrew name of Jesus of Nazareth. The Greek translation of the Hebrew name *Yeshua* ישרע was rendered Ιησου, as we find throughout the Greek New Testament. When translated into English, the New Testament Iesous became Jesus.

SEVEN

The Messiah Codes

The Name of Jesus the Nazarene and His Disciples Encoded in Isaiah 53

The central theme of the prophecies of both the Old Testament and the New Testament is God's inspired revelation of Jesus of Nazareth as the Messiah and the Son of God. A powerful indication of the validity of these codes is that these discoveries truly glorify Jesus of Nazareth in His divine roles as the Messiah, Adonai, Jehovah, and Lord. John teaches us one important spiritual test whereby we can judge any communication: "Hereby know ye the Spirit of God: Every spirit that confesseth that Jesus Christ is come in the flesh is of God" (1 John 4:2). The fact that the Bible Codes glorify Jesus Christ as the Son of God who came in the flesh to die for our sins provides strong evidence that God purposefully placed these codes into the ancient Scriptures to glorify Jesus Christ.

After my book *The Signature of God* and Yacov Rambsel's book *YESHUA* were released, they quickly became international bestsellers. However, some scholars challenged the significance of Rambsel's discovery of the name *Yeshua* encoded in virtually every major messianic prophecy in the Old Testament. Some critics claimed that since the name *Yeshua* ישוע is a relatively short name with only four Hebrew letters, it could be found by random chance at large ELS intervals almost anywhere in Hebrew literature. However, they could not explain why the name *Yeshua* would appear encoded repeatedly in small ELS intervals within dozens of major messianic prophecies throughout the Old Testament. No one has found the encoded names of any other historical figures that appear repeatedly in small ELS intervals within these key messianic passages. Only the name *Yeshua* has been found repeatedly encoded in over twenty-four messianic verses. Jewish sages, in writings such as the Talmud and the *Zohar,* agree with Christians in identifying many of these same prophecies as messianic.

Do the Yeshua Codes Point to Jesus of Nazareth?

The real question to be determined is this: Do the Yeshua codes in the messianic passages actually refer to the historic Jesus of Nazareth, or are they just a coincidence as the skeptics suggest? After pondering this question, I thought of an experiment that could settle the issue.

Some time ago I asked Rambsel to complete an exhaustive analysis of the famous messianic prophecy in Isaiah 52:13–53:12, called the Suffering Servant prophecy, to determine if it contained Bible Codes that might refer to Jesus of Nazareth. These two chapters, which should be read together as a complete passage, portray Israel's Messiah suffering and dying for our sins. Isaiah 52 reveals God's promise of blessing, and Isaiah 53, the sacrificial price of the blessing. Isaiah provides a powerful description of the Messiah as the Lamb of God and predicts many details about His death on the cross, His burial, and His resurrection—prophecies that were fulfilled seven centuries later in the person of Jesus Christ. If there were any particular passages in the Old Testament in which one might anticipate that God would place Bible Codes about Jesus Christ and His disciples, most Christians would assume that Isaiah 52–53 would be a logical place to look.

The results of Rambsel's analysis were beyond our expectations. Rambsel made a discovery that God has encoded the names of Jesus Christ and virtually every person that was associated with Him at His crucifixion. He found that not only has God encoded the name of His Messiah, Jesus, but He has also encoded *Nazarene, Messiah,* the three Marys, the names of the two high priests, *Herod, Pilate, Caesar,* and many of Christ's disciples in one prophetic passage. Furthermore, these names were encoded in Isaiah's prophecy (written in 740 B.C.) more than seven centuries before Jesus was born. Who else, other than Jesus of Nazareth, could these names refer to?

If the critics who have challenged our conclusion that the encoded name of Yeshua refers to the historical Jesus of Nazareth would examine this messianic prophecy, they would find over forty encoded names identifying virtually everyone who was associated with the crucifixion of Jesus Christ. The odds against these encoded words naming people, places, and events in the life of Jesus occurring by random chance in a similar-sized Hebrew text other than the Bible are simply staggering.

The Suffering Servant Prophecy of Isaiah 52:13–53:12

The following is the full text in English and Hebrew of this key messianic passage.

Behold, my Servant shall deal prudently, he shall be exalted and extolled, and be very high. As many were astonied at thee; his visage was so marred more than any man, and his form more than the sons of men: So shall he sprinkle many nations; the kings shall shut their mouths at him: for that which had not been told them shall they see; and that which they had not heard shall they consider. (Isaiah 52:13–15)

Who hath believed our report? and to whom is the arm of the LORD revealed? For he shall grow up before him as a tender plant, and as a root out of a dry ground: he hath no form nor comeliness; and when we shall see him, there is no beauty that we should desire him. He is despised and rejected of men; a man of sorrows, and acquainted with grief: and we hid as it were our faces from him; he was despised, and we esteemed him not. Surely he hath borne our griefs, and carried our sorrows: yet we did esteem him stricken, smitten of God, and afflicted. But he was wounded for our transgressions, he was bruised for our iniquities: the chastisement of our peace was upon him; and with his stripes we are healed. All we like sheep have gone astray; we have turned every one to his own way; and the LORD hath laid on him the iniquity of us all. He was oppressed, and he was afflicted, yet he opened not his mouth: he is brought as a lamb to the slaughter, and as a sheep before her shearers is dumb, so he openeth not his mouth. He was taken from prison and from judgment: and who shall declare his generation? for he was cut off out of the land of the living: for the transgression of my people was he stricken. And he made his grave with the wicked, and with the rich in his death; because he had done no violence, neither was any deceit in his mouth. Yet it pleased the LORD to bruise him; he hath put him to grief: when thou shalt make his soul an offering for sin, he shall see his seed, he shall prolong his days, and the pleasure of the LORD shall prosper in his hand. He shall see of the travail of his soul, and shall be satisfied: by his knowledge shall my righteous servant justify many; for he shall bear their iniquities. Therefore will I divide him a portion with the great, and he shall divide the spoil with the strong; because he hath poured out his soul unto death: and he was numbered with the transgressors; and he bare the sin of many, and made intercession for the transgressors. (Isaiah 53:1–12)

Isaiah 52:13–15

13. הנה ישכיל עבדי ירום ונשא וגבה מאד.

14. כאשר שממו עליך רבים כן_משחת
מאיש מראהו ותארו מבני אדם:

כן יזה גוים רבים עליו יקפצו מלכים 15.
פיהם כי אשרלא_ספרלהם ראו
ואשר לא_שמעו התבוננו.

Isaiah 53:1–12

מי האמין לשמעתנו וזרוע יהוה על_מי 1.
נגלתה.

כיונק לפניו וכשרש מארץ ציה לא_תאר 2.
ויעללו ולא הדר ונראהו ולא_מראה
ונחמדהו.

נבזה וחדל אישים איש מכאבות וידוע 3.
חלי וכמסתר פנים ממנו נבזה ולא חשבנהו.

אכן חלינו הוא נשא ומכאבינו סבלם 4.
ואנחנו חשבנהו נגוע מכה אלהים ומענה.

והוא מחלל מפשעינו מדכא מעונתינו 5.
מוסר שלומנו עליו ובחברתו נרפא_לנו.

כלנו כצאן תעינו איש לדרכו 6.
פנינו ויהוה הפגיע בו את עון כלנו.

נגש והוא נענה ולא יפתח_פיו כשה לטבח 7.
יובל וכרחל לפני גזזיה נאלמה ולא יפתח
פיו.

מעצר וממשפט לקח ואת_דורו מי ישוחח 8.

כי נגזר מארץ חיים מפשע עמי נגע למו.

9. ויתן את_רשעים קברו ואת_עשיר במתיו
    על לא_חמס עשה ולא מרמה בפיו.

10. ויהוה חפץ דכאו החלי אם_תשים אשם נפשו
    יראה זרע יאריך ימים וחפץ יהוה בידו יצלח.

11. מעמל נפשו יראה ישבע בדעתו יצדיק
    צדיק עבדי לרבים ועונתם הוא יסבל.

12. לכן אחלק_לו ברבים ואת_עצומים יחלק
    שלל תחת אשר הערה למות נפשו ואת_
    פשעים נמנה והוא חטא_רבים נשא ולפשעים
    יפגיע.

"Exceedingly High, Yeshua is My Strong Name."

In the last chapter I documented Yacov Rambsel's discovery of
Yeshua Shmi ישרע שמי, which occurred at a 20-letter interval
from left to right, beginning with the second Hebrew letter *yod*
י in the phrase "He shall prolong," *ya'arik* יאריך. Moreover,
as he searched this key passage more closely, Rambsel found
that starting with the fifth letter in the ninth word in Isaiah
53:11 and counting every 20th letter from left to right spells an
even longer code: *Ma 'al Yeshua Shmi Ahz* מעל ישרע שמי עז,
which means "exceedingly high, Yeshua is My strong name."
The odds against this code appearing in a prophecy about the
Messiah by random chance are astronomical.

Yeshua the Nazarene

The identification of Jesus as a Nazarene was based primarily on the fact that Jesus lived with his family until He was almost thirty in the town of Nazareth in northern Galilee, where Joseph, the husband of Jesus' mother, Mary, pursued His occupation as a carpenter. Scripture confirms this identification: "And [Jesus] came and dwelt in a city called Nazareth: that it might be fulfilled which was spoken by the prophets, He shall be called a Nazarene [נזיר]" (Matthew 2:23).

The word *Nazarene* was also used to describe a special person who was chosen for a sacred purpose and dedicated to

The Nazarene

Nazarene נזיר (every 47 letters forward) ◯

6. כלנו כצאן תעינו איש לדרכו

פנינו ויהוה הפגיע בו את עון כלנו.

7. נגש והוא נענה ולא יפתח-פיו כשה לטבח

יובל וכרחל לפני גזזיה נאלמה ולא יפתח פיו.

8. מעצר וממשפט לקח ואת-דורו מי ישוחח

כי נגזר מארץ מיים מפשע עמי נגע למו.

9. ויתן את-רשעים קברו ואת-עשיר במתיו

על לא-חמס עשה ולא מרמה בפיו.

the service of God. A Nazarite was totally dedicated to the worship of the Lord and was willing to take the serious vow of the Nazarene. Jesus' name is associated with this meaning of the word *Nazarene* because of His total commitment to His sacred calling to fulfill the will of God to redeem mankind from the curse of sin. Hannah, the mother of the prophet Samuel, dedicated her unborn son to the Lord by pledging him to the service of the Tabernacle under the terms of the vow of the Nazarene: "And she vowed a vow, and said, O Lord of hosts, if Thou wilt indeed look on the affliction of thine handmaid, and remember me, and not forget thine handmaid, but wilt give unto thine handmaid a man child, then I will give him unto the Lord all the days of his life, and there shall no razor come upon his head" (1 Samuel 1:11).

In Isaiah 53:6, starting with the third letter in the eleventh word and counting every 47th letter from right to left, we find the word *Nazarene* נזיר. Throughout Isaiah's messianic passage, the word *Nazarene* is encoded several times. This discovery of the encoded name *Nazarene* נזיר near the name *Yeshua* ישרע in the same messianic prophecy, together with the names of many of His disciples, provides powerful evidence that these Bible Codes refer to the historical Jesus of Nazareth.

Galilee

In addition, the codes reveal the place where Jesus lived for most of his life, Galilee. In Isaiah 53:7, starting with the second letter in the first word and counting every 32nd letter from left to right spells "Galilee" גליל. There are two ways in Hebrew to spell "Galilee." The first is with the *heh* ה at the end of the word, and the second is without the *heh* ה letter.

Jesus was raised in Nazareth, in a region of northern Israel called Galilee, as confirmed in Matthew 21:11: "And the multitude said, This is Jesus [Yeshua] the prophet of Nazareth of Galilee." In addition, much of His ministry was conducted at various locations surrounding the beautiful Sea of Galilee.

The Ancestors of King David and Jesus

The gospel of Luke records the genealogy of Jesus, proving that He was descended from the royal line of King David and therefore had the right to be called the king of Israel. Luke 3:32 records a significant part of the royal lineage of Jesus, beginning with King David: "Which was the son of Jesse, which was the son of Obed, which was the son of Booz [Boaz]." The names of these ancestors are also encoded in Isaiah 53:7. Starting with the second letter in the third word, which means "was afflicted" נענה and counting every 19th letter from left to right spells "Obed" Ohved עבד. The name "Obed" means "servant." It is significant that Obed was the son of Ruth and Boaz, the grandfather of King David. Jesus is called both "the Son of David" and "the suffering Servant [Obed]." In Isaiah 52:9, beginning with the first letter in the third word, which means "together" יחדו, and counting every 19th letter from left to right spells "Jesse" Yishai ישי, the son of Obed and the father of King David. The name "Jesse" means "wealthy" or "gift." Incredibly, these key ancestors of King David and Jesus of Nazareth are encoded in this messianic prophecy of Isaiah.

Three Marys and the Disciple John at the Cross

The gospel of John records that three women named Mary

Miryam מרים were present at the crucifixion of Jesus, together with His beloved disciple, John *Yochanan* יוחנן. John 19:25–27 says, "Now there stood by the cross of Jesus his mother, and his mother's sister, Mary the wife of Cleophas, and Mary Magdalene. When Jesus therefore saw his mother, and the disciple [John] standing by, whom he loved, he saith unto his mother, Woman, behold thy son! Then saith he to the disciple [John], Behold thy mother! And from that hour that disciple took her unto his own home." This moving passage reveals the profound love of Jesus for His mother, Mary, and His loyal friend, John.

When we analyze this prophecy in the Hebrew text, we find that the names of the three Marys and the disciple John are also encoded beside the name "Jesus" *Yeshua* ישוע, which is spelled out at 20-letter intervals reading left to right beginning in Isaiah 53:10. Beginning with the second Hebrew letter, *yod* י, that occurs in the phrase "He shall prolong," *ya'arik* יאריך and counting in reverse every twenty-eighth letter spells "John" יוחנן. Isaiah 52:13 says, "Behold, my servant [Yeshua] shall deal prudently, he shall be exalted and extolled, and be very high." In Isaiah 53:11, starting with the first letter in the first word and counting every 42nd letter from left to right spells "Messiah" *Mashiach* משיח. From the *mem* (מ) in the word "Messiah," counting every 23rd letter from left to right spells "Mary" מרים.

In Isaiah 53:10, all three of the encoded names of Mary use the letter *yod* (י) in the word *ya'arik* יאריך. This is the same letter *yod* (י) that forms the first letter in the encoded names "Yeshua" and "John." In Isaiah 53:10, starting with the third letter in the seventh word and counting every 6th letter from right to left spells "Mary" *Miryam* מרים. In Isaiah 53:12, starting with the 5th letter in the fourth word and counting every 44th letter from left to right again spells

"Mary" *Miryam* מרים. When we remember that John's gospel records that these four individuals were present at the crucifixion of Jesus Christ, it is incredible to find the names of the three Marys encoded in these verses alongside the encoded names "Yeshua" and "John." In addition to naming Mary, the mother of Jesus, we find that in Isaiah 53:2, starting with the second letter in the first word and counting every 210th letter from right to left, the name "Joseph" *Yoseph* יוסף, Mary's husband, is also spelled.

The following text of Isaiah's prophecy illustrates these three encoded words: the name of the disciple John *Yochanan* יוחנן and two appearances of the name "Mary"

John   יוחנן   (every 28 letters in reverse)

[note: the final two letters נן both represent the letter N]

Two Marys   מרים   (every 6th letter in reverse and every 44th letter forward)

8.   מעצר וממשפט לקח ואת-דורו מי ישוחח
כי נגזר מארץ חיים מפשע עמי נגע למו.

9.   ויתן את-רשעים קברו ואת-עשיר במתיו
על לא-חמס עשה ולא מרמה בפיו.

10.   ויהוה חפץ דכאו החלי אם-תשים אשם נפשו
יראה זרע יאריך ימים וחפץ יהוה בידו יצלח.

11.   מעמל נפשו יראה ישבע בדעתו יצדיק
צדיק עבדי לרבים ועונתם הוא יסבל.

12.   לכן אחלק-לו ברבים ואת- עצומים יחלק
שלל תחת אשר הערה למות נפשו ואת-פשעים
נמנה והוא חטא-רבים נשא ולפשעים יפגיע.

Miryam. To simplify the illustration, I have included only two of the three occurrences of the name "Mary."

The Word "Disciples" Found in Isaiah 53

In Isaiah 53:12, starting with the third letter of the second word and counting every 55th letter from left to right spells *limmudim ahnan* למדים אנן, which means "the disciples mourn." Sometimes, the letter *tav* (ת) precedes this word. In this same count of 55, but adjacent to "disciples," we find the word "priest." In Isaiah 53:5, starting with the second letter in the first word and counting every 55th letter from left to right spells "the Kohanim" (the priestly tribe) *ha'kohain* הכהן.

The Names of the Disciples Encoded before Jesus was Born

That the names of almost every one of Jesus' disciples (Judas Iscariot is one disciple excluded) are encoded within this famous messianic prophecy of Isaiah is remarkable. The list below gives the name of each disciple and the passage in which the name is encoded:

1. Peter. *Kepha* כפה.
In Isaiah 53:3, starting with the second letter in the fifth word and counting every 19th letter from right to left, the encoded word spells "Peter" *Kepha* כפה.

2. James, the son of Zebedee. *Ya'akov* יעקב.

In Isaiah 52:2, starting with the third letter in the ninth word and counting every 34th letter from left to right, the encoded word spells "James" *Ya'akov* יעקב.

3. John. The brother of the disciple James is known as "John" *Yochanan* יוחנן.

In Isaiah 53:10, starting with the fourth letter in the eleventh word and counting every 28th letter from left to right, the encoded word spells "John" *Yochanan* יוחנן.

4. Andrew. *And'drai* אנדרי.

In Isaiah 53:4, starting with the first letter in the eleventh word, which is "God" *Elohim* אלהים, and counting every 48th letter from left to right, the encoded word spells "Andrew" *And'drai* אנדרי.

5. Philip. *Pilip* פילף.

In Isaiah 53:5, starting with the third letter in the tenth word and counting every 133rd letter from left to right spells the encoded word "Philip" *Pilip* פילף.

6. Thomas. *Toma* תומא.

In Isaiah 53:2, starting with the first letter in the eighth word and counting every 35th letter from right to left, the encoded word spells "Thomas" *Toma* תומא.

7. Matthew.

There are three ways to spell the name of the disciple Matthew: *Mati* מתי, *Mattai* מתתי, and *Mattiyahu* מתתיהו. The encoded word *Mattai* מתתי is an accepted abbreviated form of *Mattiyahu* מתתיהו. In Isaiah 53:8, starting with the first letter in the twelfth word and counting every 295th letter from left to right, we find the encoded word "Matthew" *Mattai* מתתי.

8. James, son of Alphaeus. *Ben Chalipi Ya'akov* בן חלפי יעקב.
In Isaiah 52:2, starting with the fourth letter in the third word and counting every 20th letter from left to right, the encoded word spells *Ya'akov* יעקב. Two of Christ's disciples were known by the name "James" *Ya'akov* יעקב. It is fascinating that we have found the name "James" *Ya'akov* יעקב encoded twice within Isaiah 53, in recognition that there were two disciples of Christ who were named James.

9. Simon (Zelotes), the Canaanite. *Shimon hakanai* שמעון הקני.
In Isaiah 52:14, starting with the first letter in the second word and counting every 47th letter from right to left, we find the encoded word "Simon" *Shimon* שמעון.

10. Thaddaeus. *Taddai* תדי.
In Isaiah 53:12, starting with the first letter of the eighth word and counting every 50th letter from left to right, the encoded word spells "Thaddaeus" *Taddai* תדי.

11. Matthias. *Mattiyah* מתיה.
In Isaiah 53:5, starting with the fourth letter in the seventh word and counting every 11th letter from left to right spells the encoded word "Matthias" *Mattiyah* מתיה.

Matthias was the last disciple, chosen by lot by the elders of the early Church to replace the dead traitor Judas Iscariot, whose guilt in betraying Jesus Christ caused him to commit suicide. Luke, the writer of the book of Acts,

The Names of Three of Christ's Disciples
Thomas, Peter and Andrew

Thomas *Toma* תומא (every 35 letters in reverse)

Peter *Kepha* כפה (every 19 letters)

Andrew And'drahi אנדרי (every 48 letters)

1. מן האמין לשמעתנו וזרוע יהוה על-מי נגלתה.

2. ויעל כיונק לפניו וכשרש מארץ ציה לא-תאר
   לו ולא הדר ונראהו ולא-מראה ונחמדהו.

3. נבזה וחדל אישים איש מכאבות וידוע
   חלי וכמסתר פנים ממנו נבזה ולא חשבנהו.

4. אכן חלינו הוא נשא ומכאבינו סבלם
   ואנחנו חשבנהו נגוע מכה אלהים ומענה.

records how Matthias was actually chosen: "And they gave forth their lots; and the lot fell upon Matthias [מתיה]; and he was numbered with the eleven apostles" (Acts 1:26). It is noteworthy that in the early Church an essential qualification for choosing a disciple to replace the deceased Judas Iscariot was that he had to have personally witnessed the ministry of Jesus Christ and His supernatural resurrection (Acts 1:21–26). The eyewitness requirement was established so that each disciple could personally testify to the life of Christ—from His baptism to His death and resurrection from the dead and, finally, to His ascension to heaven.

The Names of Israel's Two High Priests

The Names of Israel's Two High Priests

Caiaphas *Kayafa* כיפה (every 41 letters forward)

Annas *Ahnan* ענן (every 42 letters forward)

15. כן יזה גוים רבים עליו יקפצו מלכים פיהם כי אשר
לא-ספר להם ראו ואשר לא-שמעו התבוננו.

1. מי האמין לשמעתנו וזרוע יהוה על-מי נגלתה.

2. ויעל כיונק לפניו וכשרש מארץ ציה לא-תאר
לו ולא הדר ונראהו ולא-מראה ונחמדהו.

3. נבזה וחדל אישים איש מכאבות וידוע
חלי וכמסתר פנים ממנו נבזה ולא חשבנהו.

4. אכן חלינו הוא נשא ומכאבינו סבלם
ואנחנו חשבנהו נגוע מכה אלהים ומענה.

Jesus' Trial and the Names of the Two High Priests

When we examine the encoded information about those in power at the time of the Crucifixion, we discover the encoded names of Israel's two high priests at that time. Starting with the third letter in the seventh word in Isaiah 52:15, counting every 41st letter from left to right spells "Caiaphas" *Kayafa* כיפה, the name of the high priest of Israel who was named in the Gospel accounts of the trial of Jesus and whose tomb Israeli archeologists discovered in

1991. In Isaiah 53:3, starting with the fifth letter in the sixth word and counting every 45th letter from right to left spells "Annas" *Ahnan* ענן, the former high priest and the uncle of Caiaphas. The New Testament reveals the names of both high priests in Luke 3:2: "Annas and Caiaphas being the high priests, the word of God came unto John the son of Zacharias in the wilderness." According to John 19:15, the high (chief) priests were leaders in the Sanhedrin trial in the Temple that led to the crucifixion of Jesus: "But they cried out, Away with him, away with him, crucify him. Pilate saith unto them, Shall I crucify your King? The chief priests answered, We have no king but Caesar [the Roman]."

The Pharisees, the Levites, King Herod, Rome, and Caesar

The Pharisees and King Herod were also involved in the Crucifixion, and we see their names encoded in Isaiah 53. In verse 9, starting with the second letter in the fourteenth word and counting every 64th letter from left to right, we find the word "Pharisee" *pahrush* פרוש. These Jewish religious leaders were a strong force both in the Temple and in the broader Israeli society. They encouraged people to follow the strict religious laws of the Scriptures and the written and oral traditions that were based on the teachings of their rabbis over the centuries. It is amazing to note that in Isaiah 53:6, starting with the first letter in the fourth word and counting every 29th letter from left to right, we also find the encoded words "the man Herod" *ish Herod* איש הורד.

In Isaiah 53:11, starting with the first letter of the second word and counting every 14th letter from left to right spells the Hebrew word "Levis" *Levim* לוים, a code that clearly identifies the Temple priests, chosen from the Jewish tribe of Levi, who joined in the attack on Jesus. In addition, starting with the second letter in the thirteenth word in Isaiah 53:9 and counting every 7th letter from left to right the encoded letters spell "the evil Roman city" *rah eer Romi* רע עיר רומי, a code that identifies the Roman Empire, the political power that ruled the known world and had ordered the death of Jesus. The Jewish authorities did not possess the legal power to inflict a death sentence upon any offender found guilty in their Sanhedrin court in the Temple. The only way a death sentence could be carried out in Judea at that time was to find a Roman law that the prisoner had also broken and to then appeal to the Roman governor to sentence the person to death under the laws of Rome.

The Gentile soldiers of the Roman Empire who were present at the Crucifixion represented both the Roman Caesar (Tiberius) and the Gentile world, who also rejected the claims of Jesus as the Son of God and, thus, were spiritually complicit in the execution of God's Messiah. In this sense, all of humanity was represented at the crucifixion of the Lamb of God, Jesus Christ. In Isaiah 53:11, starting with the fourth letter in the seventh word and counting every 194th letter from left to right, we find the encoded words *Kaisar ahmail ovaid* קיסר עמל אבד, which mean "wicked, Caesar wretched [perish]," or alternatively phrased as "wicked Caesar, to perish." It is interesting to note that the Roman Caesar Tiberius died within five years following the death of Jesus Christ.

Jesus Christ: The Atonement Lamb and the Light of the World

The gospel of John records that John the Baptist received a profound revelation of Christ as the Atonement Lamb of God when Jesus came to be baptized by him in the Jordan River. "The next day John seeth Jesus coming unto him, and saith, Behold the Lamb of God, which taketh away the sin of the world" (John 1:29). In Isaiah 52:12, starting with the second letter in the twelfth word and counting every 19th letter from left to right spells "from the Atonement Lamb" *me'kippur tela* מכפר טלא.

In Isaiah 53:5, starting with the seventh letter in the fifth word and counting every twentieth letter from right to left, "lamp of the Lord" *ner Adonai* נר יהוה is spelled. This encoded word is adjacent to *Yeshua* ישרע at a 20-letter interval. The gospel of John affirms repeatedly that Jesus Christ is the true light of the world: "Then spake Jesus again unto them, saying, I am the light of the world: he that followeth me shall not walk in darkness, but shall have the light of life" (John 8:12).

The Messianic Title "Shiloh"

In Isaiah 53:9, starting with the second letter in the eleventh word and counting every 54th letter from right to left spells *Shiloh* שילה. Both Jewish and Christian scholars acknowledge that the word *Shiloh* is a clear prophetic title of the coming Messiah. In Genesis 49:10, Moses recorded the deathbed prophecy of the patriarch Jacob: "The sceptre shall not depart from Judah, nor a lawgiver from between his feet, until Shiloh

The Name of Jesus and His Messianic Title — Shiloh

Jesus - Yeshua ישוע (every 20 letters in reverse)

Shiloh שילה (every 54 letters forward)

9. ויתן את-רשעים קברו ואת-עשיר במתיו
על לא-חמס עשה ולא מרמה בפיו.
10. ויהוה חפץ דכאו החלי אם-תשים אשם נפשו
יראה זרע יאריך ימים וחפץ יהוה בידו יצלח.
11. מעמל נפשו יראה ישבע בדעתו יצדיק
צדיק עבדי לרבים ועונתם הוא יסבל.
12. לכן אחלק-לו ברבים ואת- עצומים יחלק
שלל תחת אשר הערה למות נפשו ואת-פשעים
נמנה והוא חטא-רבים נשא ולפשעים יפגיע.

come; and unto him [Yeshua] shall the gathering of the people be." This famous prophecy clearly identified the coming Messiah as "Shiloh." The discovery of the word *Shiloh* encoded beside the name *Yeshua* in Isaiah 53 provides powerful evidence of the identity of Jesus of Nazareth in this passage.

Jesus the Messiah and the Feast of Passover

In addition, the words *Yeshua* and *Messiah* are encoded in this key passage. In Isaiah 53:8, starting with the third letter in the second word and counting every 65th letter from left to right spells "Messiah" *Mashiach* משיח. At the same interval count, but starting with the third letter in the tenth word of verse 10, which is the *ayin* (ע), every 65th letter from left to right spells *Yeshua* ישוע. Also, the word "Passover" is found encoded in Isaiah 53:10. Beginning at the third letter of the thirteenth word, at an interval of every 62 letters in reverse, the word "Passover" *Peh'sakh* פסח is spelled.

The Prophetic Symbols at the Passover Supper: The Bread and Wine

Two other words that also share the same interval count are the words "bread" and "wine." In Isaiah 53:1, starting with the fifth letter in the eighth word and counting every 210th letter from right to left spells "the bread" *ha'lachem* הלחם, an encoded word that may refer to the powerful symbol of the bread that Jesus used at the Last Supper to refer to His body, which was broken for our sins. Another group of Hebrew letters at the same 210-letter interval spells the word "wine" *yeyin* יין, the other symbol used by Jesus at His last Passover Supper in the Upper Room to symbolize His blood, which was shed for our sins. The word "wine" is spelled out in reverse at a 210-letter interval, beginning with the second letter in the eleventh word and counting from right to left.

The names "Jonah" and "water" are also encoded close together in this passage. In Isaiah 52:4, starting with the fourth letter in the sixth word and counting every 19th letter from left to right spells "Jonah" יונה. A few verses later, in Isaiah 52:7, starting with the first letter in the ninth word and counting every 19th letter from left to right spells "water" מים. The prophet Jonah was placed in the water to awaken him to God's command to preach to his enemies, the Ninevites. These codes revealing "Jonah" and "water" remind us of the history of the prophet Jonah, who was "in the belly of the fish three days and three nights." Jesus used Jonah's experience as a prophetic symbol of His own death and resurrection.

Those Who Watched the Crucifixion from Afar

The gospel of Mark gives us the names of three women who were present at the Crucifixion: "There were also women looking on afar off: among whom was Mary Magdalene, and Mary the mother of James the less and of Joses, and Salome" (Mark 15:40). The names of these same three women are encoded in the Suffering Servant prophecy. In Isaiah 52:15, starting with the third letter in the sixteenth word and counting every 113th letter from right to left spells "Salome" *Shalomit* שלמית. In verse 13, starting with the fourth letter in the second word and counting every 149th letter from right to left spells "Joses" *Yosai* יוסי. Joses was apparently a son of Jesus' mother, Mary, and, therefore, His half brother. According to Mark 15:40, both Marys were weeping at the crucifixion of Jesus. Encoded in Isaiah 52:15, starting with the fifth letter in the eighteenth word and counting every 13th letter from left to right spells the words "the Marys weep bitterly" *na'ar Miryam be'ku abhor* נאר מרים בכו. In Isaiah 53:9, starting with the first letter in the third word and counting every 28th letter from right to left spells "tremble Mary" *rahal Miryam* רעל מרים. The letters adjacent to the above codes spell "the blessed" *habarucha* הברוכה. Mary, the mother of Jesus, was called "blessed" in the gospel of Luke: "And the angel came in unto her [Mary], and said, Hail, thou that art highly favoured, the Lord is with thee: blessed [ברוכה] art thou among women" (Luke 1:28).

Thus far, we have found encoded words naming virtually every one of the people associated with the crucifixion of Jesus, in addition to many others who were present during His remarkable life and ministry.

The Cross and the Passover Feast

In Isaiah 53:10, starting with the third letter in the second word and counting every 52nd letter from right to left spells "cross" צלב. In the same word, beginning with the first letter and counting every 104th letter from right to left spells "Passover" פסח. In Isaiah 52:14, starting with the third letter in the sixth word and counting every 26th letter from left to right spells "my feast [my sacrifice]" *Chaggai* חגי. After sharing His last Passover Supper with His disciples in the Upper Room, Jesus was betrayed by Judas and taken to a series of trials. His crucifixion took place the next afternoon on the day of the Passover Feast, known as *Chaggai* חגי.

The Time and Place of Christ's Crucifixion

There is a code discovery in Isaiah that names the actual month of Christ's crucifixion, Aviv, and the place of Christ's sacrifice for our sins. Jesus was crucified on the day of the Passover Feast, which took place annually on the fifteenth day of the Jewish month of Nisan (also known as the month of Aviv). Mount Moriah, the Temple Mount, is the place where God provided a ram as a substitute sacrifice in the place of Abraham's son Isaac. This also was the place where God commanded King David to prepare for the building of the Temple, later built by his son Solomon.

Mount Moriah is a long mountain ridge that begins in the south of Jerusalem and continues northward past the northern city walls to the site of Golgotha, where Jesus was crucified outside the city walls, just north of the Damascus Gate. The book of Hebrews confirms the Gospel account that Christ's death took place outside the city walls: "Wherefore Jesus also, that he might sanctify the people with his own blood, suffered without the gate" (Hebrews 13:12).

In Isaiah 52:1, starting with the third letter in the eighth word and counting every 27th letter from right to left spells *aviv ve'moriah* אביב ומריה, which means "Aviv of Mount Moriah." The adjacent letters spell *rosh* ראש, which means "the first" or "the head of the year." The first month of the religious year was the month Nisan-Aviv, the month of Passover, when Jesus was crucified.

"Let Him Be Crucified"

Over one thousand years before the birth of Jesus, the psalmist David wrote about the future death of the Messiah. His prophetic psalm foretells the tragic crucifixion of Christ: "The assembly of the wicked have enclosed me: they pierced my hands and my feet" (Psalm 22:16). Incredibly, in Isaiah 52:10 we find the word "pierce" encoded. Starting with the third letter in the fifteenth word, which means "in His hands" בידו, and counting every 92 letters from left to right, the word "pierce" *dahkar* דקר is spelled in reverse.

"LET HIM BE CRUCIFIED"

Jesus Is My Name   Yeshua Shmi   ישוע שמי   (every 20 letters in reverse)

Let Him Be Crucified   Yitz'tzah'laiv   יצלב   (every 15 letters forward)

8.   מעצר וממשפט לקח ואת-דורו מי ישוחח
      כי נגזר מארץ חיים מפשע עמי נגע למו.

9.   ויתן את-רשעים קברו ואת-עשיר במתיו
      על לא-חמס עשה ולא מרמה בפיו.

10.   ויהוה חפץ דכאו החלי אם-תשים אשם נפשו
      יראה זרע יאריך ימים וחפץ יהוה בידו יצלח.

Both the Roman and the Jewish leaders joined together to crucify Jesus of Nazareth. The gospel of Matthew records the terrible moment when the Roman governor decided on Christ's death. "Pilate saith unto them, What shall I do then with Jesus which is called Christ? They all say unto him, Let him be crucified" (Matthew 27:22). The prophet Isaiah foretold this tragic series of events seven centuries before they occurred. "He was taken from prison and from judgment: and who shall declare his generation? for he was cut off out of the land of the living: for the transgression of my people was he stricken" (Isaiah 53:8). Perhaps the most noteworthy code discovery in this passage is the fact that this exact phrase was encoded in Isaiah's prophecy. Starting with the second letter in the sixth word of Isaiah 53:8 and counting every 15th letter right to left spells "let Him be crucified" *yitz'tzahlaiv* יצלב.

Can the unbiased reader have any remaining doubt that the Bible Codes identify Jesus of Nazareth as the Messiah and Son of God who died for our sins?

The Signature of God

In 1996, I wrote a book, *The Signature of God*, that explores the fascinating evidence from archeology, science, medicine, fulfilled biblical prophecy, and the Bible Codes that proves the supernatural origin of the Bible. My thesis was that God had, in effect, written His authenticating signature on the inspired pages of His Holy Word by means of this supernatural evidence in the text, which no unaided human could have created. I was thrilled when Yacov Rambsel faxed me his discovery of a code that contained the words *me'chatimo* מחתימו, which mean "his signature." In Isaiah 52:7, starting with the fourth letter, the final *mem* מ, in the Hebrew word *shalom* שלום, the eighth word, and counting every 49th letter from right to left spells "his signature" *me'chatimo* מחתימו. The Hebrew letters מ and מ are variations of the same letter. These codes surely are the signature of God on the pages of His Word.

The final pages of this chapter contain a detailed summary of the major codes in Isaiah's prophecy that name virtually everyone associated with the life and ministry of Jesus. This list should be a convenience for the reader and an aid to those students of the Bible who wish to check out these Bible Codes for themselves, using a Hebrew-English Interlinear Bible.

Jesus and His Disciples Found Encoded in Isaiah 52 and 53

Encoded Word	Hebrew	Begins	Word	Letter	Interval
Yeshua Shmi	ישרע שמי	Isa. 53:10	11	4	(-20)
Nazarene	נזיר	Isa. 53:6	11	3	(47)
Messiah	משיח	Isa. 53:11	1	1	(-42)
Shiloh	שילה	Isa. 53:12	21	4	(19)
Passover	פסח	Isa. 53:10	13	3	(-62)
Galilee	גליל	Isa. 53:7	1	2	(-32)
Herod	הורד	Isa. 53:6	4	1	(-29)
Caesar	קיסר	Isa. 53:11	7	4	(-194)
The evil Roman city	רע עיר רומי	Isa. 53:9	13	2	(-7)
Caiaphas	כיפה	Isa. 52:15	7	3	(41)
Annas	ענן	Isa. 53:3	6	5	(-45)
Mary	מרים	Isa. 53:11	1	1	(-23)
Mary	מרים	Isa. 53:10	7	3	(6)
Mary	מרים	Isa. 53:9	13	3	(44)
The Disciples	למדים	Isa. 53:12	2	3	(-55)
Peter	כפה	Isa. 53:10	11	5	(-14)
Matthew	מתתי	Isa. 53:8	12	1	(-295)

John	יוחנן	Isa. 53:10	11	4	(-28)
Andrew	אנדרי	Isa. 53:4	11	1	(-48)
Philip	פילף	Isa. 53:5	10	3	(-133)
Thomas	תומא	Isa. 53:2	8	1	(35)
James	יעקב	Isa. 52:2	9	3	(-34)
James	יעקב	Isa. 52:2	3	4	(-20)
Simon	שמעון	Isa. 52:14	2	1	(47)
Thaddaeus	תדי	Isa. 53:12	9	1	(-50)
Matthias	מתיה	Isa. 53:5	7	4	(-11)
Let Him be crucified	יצלב	Isa. 53:8	6	2	(15)
Cross	צלב	Isa. 53:10	2	3	(52)
Pierce	דקר	Isa. 52:10	15	3	(-92)
Lamp of the Lord	נר יהוה	Isa. 53:5	5	7	(20)
His signature	מחתימו	Isa. 52:7	8	4	(49)
The Bread	הלחם	Isa. 53:12	2	3	(26)
Wine	יין	Isa. 53:5	11	2	(210)
Zion	ציון	Isa. 52:14	6	1	(45)
Moriah	ומריה	Isa. 52:7	4	5	(153)
Obed	עבד	Isa. 53:7	3	2	(-19)
Jesse	ישי	Isa. 52:9	3	1	(-19)
Seed	זרע	Isa. 52:15	2	2	(-19)
Water	מים	Isa. 52:7	9	1	(-19)
Levites	לוים	Isa. 54:3	3	6	(19)
Pharisee	פרוש	Isa. 53:9	14	2	(-64)
From the Atonement Lamb	מכפר טלא	Isa. 52:12	12	2	(-19)
Joseph	יוסף	Isa. 53:2	1	2	(210)

Rambsel found the forty-one encoded words associated with the life and ministry of Jesus, including the names of

His disciples, without the aid of a computer search program, by manually searching Isaiah's messianic prophecy. However, I completed a search using a Bible Codes search program to see if I could find a similar group of Bible Codes about Jesus and His disciples in a comparable passage in the Torah. The following list of Bible Codes reveals the names of Christ's disciples (including Matthias), plus several other significant words, including *Nazarene, Galilee, Shiloh, Mary,* and *"Let Him be crucified"* surrounding Exodus 30:16.

Jesus of Nazareth and His Disciples in Exodus 30

Encoded Word	Hebrew	Begins	Word	Letter	Interval
Yeshua	ישוע	Ex. 30:16	19	1	(12)
Nazarene	נזיר	Ex. 30:16	15	3	(8)
Messiah	משיח	Ex. 30:13	12	3	(60)
Shiloh	שילה	Ex. 30:14	7	1	(40)
Passover	פסח	Ex. 30:9	7	4	(-9)
Galilee	גליל	Ex. 28:42	5	1	(-21)
Mary	מרים	Ex. 30:15	7	2	(60)
Mary	מרים	Ex. 30:16	13	1	(61)
Mary	מרים	Ex. 30:17	5	3	(92)
Peter	כפה	Ex. 30:16	17	3	(19)
Matthew	מתתי	Ex. 30:15	6	1	(-19)
John	יוחנן	Ex. 29:19	9	1	(14)
Andrew	אנדרי	Ex. 29:39	10	2	(79)
Philip	פילך	Ex. 29:24	9	4	(50)

Thomas	תומא	Ex. 30:18	14	4	(11)
James	יעקב	Ex. 30:7	6	2	(-59)
Simon	שמעון	Ex. 29:19	7	3	(-39)
Nathanael	נתנאל	Ex. 30:4	8	2	(-100)
Judas	יהודה	Ex. 29:13	9	2	(24)
Thaddaeus	תדי	Ex. 30:16	2	2	(32)
Matthias	מתיה	Ex. 30:20	8	2	(20)
Let Him be crucified	יצלב	Ex. 30:20	1	1	(8)

EIGHT

A Response to Critics of the Yeshua Codes

There are five types of ELS word patterns that may be found in a given text:

1. *accidental ELS words,* which have no meaning;

2. *legitimate multiple ELS codes* (e.g., the "Famous Rabbis"), which can be statistically demonstrated to be so unlikely to occur by random chance in a particular small passage that researchers can conclude that these ELS words were placed within the text by an intelligent mind;

3. *multiple low-interval ELS codes* located in a specific passage of the Scriptures dealing with the same subject as the encoded words (e.g., the twenty-five trees found in Genesis 2);

4. *groups of encoded words that describe specific details of future historical events* that occurred centuries after the Bible was written. It appears extremely probable that the ELS words were deliberately inserted into a text and are

therefore instances of a genuine Bible Code (e.g., Hitler, Holocaust). However, such ELS codes must be analyzed carefully to see if comparable groups of ELS encoded words can be found in a nonbiblical text.

5. *single low-interval ELS codes* (e.g., *Yeshua*) that appear in a specific, thematically linked passage (e.g., a major messianic prophecy). Because there is only one target word in such cases, we cannot demonstrate statistically the probability that such a word appears in that specific verse by chance. However, when Yacov Rambsel demonstrates that the name *Yeshua* appears at low ELS intervals in dozens of messianic prophecies, most people conclude that these Bible Codes are placed in the Scriptures purposefully.

In several instances Rambsel found several ELS words encoded together in a significant phrase, such as *Yeshua Shmi* "Yeshua is My name" or *Haim dam Yeshua* "Behold the blood of Yeshua." It is statistically unlikely that these multiple ELS words about Yeshua appear in these messianic prophecies by random chance. The article "A Statistical Study on the Yeshua Codes," published on the Internet by Guy Cramer and Lori Eldridge, calculates the statistical probability of several of Rambsel's discoveries.

Criticism of the Yeshua Codes and My Response to the Critics

Since Rambsel and I have published Rambsel's discovery about the Yeshua codes, a number of Israeli code researchers have stated that the Yeshua codes are not genuine ELS codes.

They suggest that the finding of the name *Yeshua* in these messianic prophecies is accidental and meaningless because it does not meet the exacting statistical criteria of the Israelis' "Famous Rabbis" experiment. My response to these critics has been that they themselves consider this type of ELS code significant, as exemplified in their reporting of Bible Codes such as "Sadat," "Hitler," and the "twenty-five trees." By their own admission, these codes cannot be statistically verified in the same manner as the "Famous Rabbis" codes.

It is interesting to note that some of these critics of the Yeshua codes now reject every ELS code that cannot be statistically verified by the more exacting criteria favored by the Israeli code researchers. To these critics, it doesn't matter if anyone else discovers significant ELS codes. The researchers and critics who use the Israeli statistical computer analysis code research, such as Rabbi Daniel Mechanic, Dr. Rips, and Dr. Gans, now automatically disqualify every ELS code that hasn't been found with an a priori search (a search in which you define in advance of the experiment what you expect to find). They refuse to call any other type of ELS discovery a valid code, and even go so far as to claim that an ELS code cannot be analyzed statistically if it falls outside their rigid criteria of analysis.

But how can anyone arbitrarily limit the ELS codes that God may have placed within the text of the Holy Scriptures? If God placed ELS codes within the text of the Scriptures, then we must examine all possibilities to determine if the codes we find are valid and purposeful.

These critics have attacked and challenged Yacov Rambsel and me on our supposedly "unscientific research" regarding the Yeshua codes and our so-called "deceptive" attempts to proselytize Jews. They have issued a public attack on the Internet and in their seminars by claiming that our ELS discoveries about the Yeshua codes are not genuine. They make a convincing argument that large interval ELS codes are suspect because many meaningless ELS codes can be found at such distances. Most people familiar with the codes phenomenon would agree that words that appear at large ELS intervals should be eliminated from serious code research unless the discovered codes are remarkable in some manner. This is why I use examples in this book of Yeshua codes that occur only at fairly low ELS intervals.

The critics claim that I attempt, by "constantly mentioning the foremost Codes experts in the world: Doron Witztum, Harold Gans and Jeffrey Satinover," to "establish credibility" for myself and the Yeshua codes. My response is that I mention the code discoveries of these Israeli and Jewish researchers only because I admire the significance of their research. One critic uses my statement "Harold Gans confirmed the existence of these codes" to suggest that I applied Dr. Gans's statement to Rambsel's discovery of the Yeshua codes and, thereby, deliberately misled people.

These attacks have no basis in truth whatsoever. In my lectures and books I have clearly separated the ELS codes confirmed by the Israeli researchers, such as Drs. Rips and Gans, from the Yeshua code discoveries that Yacov Rambsel and I have reported. In my book *The Signature of God,* the ELS codes discovered by the Israeli researchers are discussed in chapter 10.[1] None of the three Jewish code researchers mentioned in that chapter are mentioned in chapter 11, the chapter which deals with Rambsel's discovery of the Yeshua codes. In fact, I had completed writing chapter 10 months before I had even heard about Rambsel's discovery of the Yeshua codes.

Moreover, both Rambsel and I document our ELS code discoveries with the specific Bible chapter, verse, and word so that any reader with a Hebrew-English Interlinear Bible can verify the existence of every one of the ELS codes that we claim are significant. In our examples, we usually cite the beginning letter, the direction of the encoded word, and the ELS interval. These specifics make it possible for anyone to verify our Bible Codes.

In contrast, our critics on the Internet usually document their Bible Code discoveries with nothing more than a foot-note stating that a particular encoded word (e.g., "Buddha") begins with the 53,479th letter of Genesis, which is located in chapter 36. The minimal information provided by these researchers does not allow the average reader to verify a single one of the codes that the critics use to rebut the Yeshua code discoveries. Very few readers possess the specific software programs that can confirm the critics' claims. Moreover, the critics seldom document the ELS interval of the encoded word. These factors make verifying the critics' counterclaims nearly impossible or, at least, exceedingly difficult since a researcher is forced to search the whole of the Old Testament to locate the critics' examples.

It is significant that no Jewish researcher (including our critics) has denied that the Yeshua codes exist in the specific passages that we have cited. Many pastors and rabbis with seminary or Yeshiva training in Hebrew have examined the text of the Hebrew Bible and verified our documented claims.

The critics have published on the Internet that they found the names *Mohammed, Koresh,* and *Buddha* encoded in the messianic prophecies where we found *Yeshua* encoded. However, they do not document where they found these names, or the intervals at which they were encoded, so that other researchers can verify their claims. They state in their critique, *Yeshua Codes: Uses and Abuses,* that they only search for codes at letter intervals of 1,000 or less. Such a broad interval search, however, produces a staggering number of letter combinations.

In contrast, the intervals in the Yeshua codes that Rambsel and I have published range from a high interval of 612 letters (two occurrences) to a low interval of only 2 letters. Fifty of the seventy-two Yeshua codes have intervals of 50 letters or less.

In their comments disputing the significance of Rambsel's discovery of the encoded phrase "behold the blood of Yeshua," the critics claim that they have discovered codes such as the "blood of Mohammed" and the "blood of Koresh." However, attempts by other researchers (myself included) to verify these discoveries suggest that the critics' codes are never found at statistically low ELS intervals. In contrast, Rambsel's discovery of the coded phrase "behold the blood of Yeshua" is found at a 3-letter interval, beginning in Leviticus 21:10. Moreover, this verse of Scripture is highly significant because it describes the consecration and anointing of the high priest of Israel: "And he that is the high priest among his brethren, upon whose head the anointing oil was poured, and that is consecrated to put on the garments, shall not uncover his head, nor rend his clothes" (Leviticus 21:10).

It is equally significant that Rambsel found many Yeshua codes in precisely those messianic verses where Christians would expect to find them if God had placed such codes in the Bible. If several Christian Bible students were asked to identify a dozen of the most likely verses in the Old Testament where God might encode the Hebrew name of Jesus, I believe almost everyone would pick the following passages: Genesis 3:15, Psalm 22:16, Psalm 41:8–9, Isaiah 41:7–8, Isaiah 53:8–11, Isaiah 61:1, Daniel 9:26, Zechariah 9:9–10, Micah 5:1, and Zechariah 11:12. Christians generally recognize these verses as clear messianic prophecies that were historically fulfilled in the life and death of Jesus of Nazareth. Rambsel discovered that each one of these messianic passages contains the encoded names *Yeshua* and *Messiah*. Significantly, 70 percent of these codes are located at intervals of less than 26 letters. If the critics wish to prove that our Yeshua codes are meaningless coincidences, they should produce Bible Codes of the names of other men at intervals of less than 26 letters that are encoded in the same messianic passages.

In the historical overview of the code phenomenon, we noted the initial discovery of the codes in the medieval period, followed by Rabbi Weissmandl's discoveries in this century. All of these were the third and fourth types of codes listed on the first page of this chapter (i.e., codes that did not meet the criteria of the "Famous Rabbis" experiment). Then we explored the discoveries in Israel in the last decade or so. In discussing the Yeshua codes, we stated that these codes cannot be subjected to statistical analysis because the nature of their appearance in specific and well-known messianic passages does not lend itself to the same standard of statistical analysis used to verify the "Famous Rabbis" experiment. However, the assertion that no codes have significance unless they meet the specific mathematical and statistical criteria used in the "Famous Rabbis" experiment is simply wrong, especially when considering that in the past many of the same critics have supported similar types of nonstatistically verifiable codes such as *Holocaust, Sadat,* and *Rabin.*

These critics claim that "if it cannot be proven that a particular 'code' was deliberately placed in a document, and a statistical evaluation shows it to be meaningless, their 'existence' cannot—and should not—be used as proof of anything."

A careful reading of their critique reveals that this is their basic and fundamental criticism of Rambsel's discovery of the Yeshua codes. They correctly point out that the ELS codes revealing "Hitler," "Sadat," "Rabin," and the many Yeshua codes cannot meet the statistical criteria in the same way that the "Famous Rabbis" experiment could be verified. However, the claim by these critics that this means that the third, fourth, and fifth types of codes listed on the first page of this chapter are therefore meaningless is both illogical and inconsistent. A particular ELS encoded word or words can be meaningful based on their placement in a particular passage of the Bible even though the code does not meet the specific statistical criteria demonstrated in the "Famous Rabbis" experiment.

Many of the Israeli critics participate in or support the teaching of the codes by the Aish Ha Torah/Discovery Seminar. I have received numerous audiotapes, publications, and reports from those attending these seminars. These sources, in addition to numerous newspaper articles, confirm that the Aish Ha Torah/Discovery Seminars teach participants about the phenomenon of the Bible Codes, including the "Famous Rabbis" experiment and many of the following code discoveries: *Torah, Sadat,* the Rabin assassination, *Hitler,* the twenty-five trees (in Genesis 2), *Aaron* (in Leviticus 1), the ancestors of King David (in Genesis 38), *Hanukkah, Hasmoneans,* and *Zedekiah.*

In their brochure, Aish Ha Torah calls these other codes "impressive," while noting that they are not statistically verified. The purpose of these Aish Ha Torah/Discovery Seminars is to prove that the Bible is inspired by God because no human could have produced these complex codes containing knowledge of future events. Two such examples of their discoveries are 1) the names of the ancestors of King David encoded in the Genesis 38 account of Judah and Tamar, and 2) the encoded words *Torah* and *Temple* in the Genesis 28 account of Jacob's dream of the staircase to heaven at "the house of God"—both of which are discoveries that are statistically unverifiable.

Obviously, most of the code examples taught by Aish Ha Torah/Discovery Seminars do not meet the special statistical standards of the "Famous Rabbis" experiment. Does that mean that their illustration of these Bible Codes about Hitler and Sadat, for example, demonstrates "a complete misunderstanding of the 'codes methodology,' how it works, and what can and cannot be asserted concerning them?" Obviously not. Aish Ha Torah/Discovery Seminars, which are supported by the Yeshua code critics, promote these codes, in addition to the "Famous Rabbis" experiment, as examples of the code phenomenon. Aish Ha Torah/Discovery Seminars teach that these other codes, even though not statistically significant, are of importance.

It is intellectually dishonest, therefore, for these critics to claim that we Christian researchers are "irresponsible" and are engaging in "fraudulent and deceptive" behavior when we report that it is significant that the name *Yeshua* is encoded at low intervals in virtually every one of the major messianic prophecies. I can understand why they might be angry and upset at the discovery of these Yeshua codes in messianic passages. Nevertheless, it is illogical and intellectually dishonest for the critics to vilify Christians for reporting the significance of the Yeshua codes, while, at the same time, they support the lecturers of the Aish Ha Torah/Discovery Seminar who report the significance of Bible Codes similar in type to the Yeshua codes.

Anyone who examines the phenomenon of the Bible Codes for any length of time will recognize the difference between codes that can be statistically verified and those that are "significant" because they occur in a particular passage of Scripture. While anyone can correctly state that these "other" codes are not statistically verified, most observers, including the lecturers of Aish Ha Torah, still conclude that they are of sufficient interest to justify their publication as meaningful and significant. Obviously, each person must examine the data and draw his or her own conclusions.

Finally, these critics reject the Yeshua codes because, they say, the name *Yeshua* appears so often it is meaningless. First, the critics acknowledge that the name *Yeshua* appears in all of these important messianic passages. It is true the name *Yeshua* is encoded frequently in the Bible, but that most likely is because He is the Messiah. The point is that the name *Yeshua* has been found at low intervals in major messianic prophecies. If the name *Yeshua* turned up encoded in only a few of these critically significant passages, it would not have been significant, and we would not have presented this discovery.

Claims that the Codes Reveal that Yeshua Is a False Messiah and My Response

Some of the critics of the Yeshua codes have claimed on the Internet and in their seminars that they have discovered hidden ELS codes that spell *yeshua moshiach sheker* "Jesus is a false messiah." These critics teach that these codes are an indication that Jesus should be rejected by the Jews. First, we need to recognize that the name *Yeshua,* as the name of God's Messiah, naturally appears many times throughout the Old Testament. Therefore, the name *Yeshua* will inevitably be found in texts reasonably close to a number of other key words. The claim that someone has found a text where the encoded word *Yeshua* occasionally appears near the word *sheker* "false messiah," or that the name *Yeshua* sometimes occurs at the same large ELS as *sheker,* does not mean that the codes teach that Jesus is the false messiah, as some anti-Christians would like to suggest.

Moreover, contrary to the impression these critics would like to create, the phrase "Yeshua is a false messiah" is not found in ELS code anywhere in the Hebrew text of the Old Testament. Rather, the critics can only point to the fact that they have found the word *Yeshua* and the word *sheker* at equal ELS skip intervals in the Torah. They suggest that this proves that Jesus is a false messiah. This is pure nonsense. The ELS intervals are not located close together in a messianic prophecy, for example, but simply share, in this instance, a huge ELS skip interval. In other words, there is no logical or close spatial relationship between these words, as opposed to the complex group of codes in Isaiah 52 and 53 naming Jesus and His disciples. In light of the fact that Yacov

Rambsel is the primary discoverer and researcher of the Yeshua codes, I have asked him to respond to the specific allegations regarding the "false Messiah" codes.

Specific Examples of Codes that Critics Claim Reveal Yeshua is a False Messiah

Here are some specific examples of the claim that the phrase *yeshua moshiach sheker* "Jesus is the false messiah" can be found in an ELS code, together with Yacov Rambsel's reply to each claim.

(1) *Isaiah 7:1–17.* The word *moshiach* messiah appears at 11-letter intervals from right to left, beginning with the letter *mem* מ in *melech* in 7:1. Critics point out that *Yeshua* is encoded at an interval of 27 letters left to right beginning with the *yod* י in *bochori* in 7:4. The critics then point to the three-letter word *sheker* שקר (spelled *shin, kaf, reish*) that appears in this passage beginning with the *shin* ש in the word *Damesek* in 7:8, counting the next two letters. They claim that the two words are closely connected, but obviously they are not.

Yacov Rambsel's reply:

The problem with the above statement is that a letter is missing from the text as provided by this source. This has been verified by three different Hebrew texts, including the Masoretic text. Unfortunately, one of the computer programs varies the spelling of words in this Hebrew text from the authorized Masoretic text in this passage. This mistake nullifies the critics' entire analysis.

However, there is an interesting reason why the word *sheker* (false) appears in this passage. Isaiah 7:8 declares: "For the head of Syria is Damascus, and the head of Damascus is Rezin; and within threescore and five years shall Ephraim be broken, that it be not a people." The Hebrew words "Damesek" and "Rezin" provide additional insights. The third, fourth, and fifth letters from the right of the above spells "false," "liar," "perverse," or *sheker*. These words reveal the agenda of the nation Syria in its approach to Israel since 1948.

(2) *Isaiah 7:15*. Some critics claim that the Hebrew letters in *Yeshua* beginning with the letter *yod* י in Isaiah 7:1 and skipping forward at intervals of 245 letters spell *Yeshua*, ending at 7:15. Beginning with the letter *shin* שׁ in the word *Israel* in 7:1, they count forward at a skip interval of 140 letters, spelling *sheker*, which ends in 7:5. Then, they claim the word *sheker* intersects the word *Yeshua* and *moshiach*.

Yacov Rambsel's reply:

I did the analysis, and I came up with an entirely different phrase. Starting with the *shin* שׁ in the word "Israel" in Isaiah 7:1 and counting every 140th letter in both directions (forward and reverse) spells *Ôhamah'shak rosh'*, which means "the head steward." Yeshua (Jesus) is the head steward and Servant to all mankind. If you separate the *qof* ק letter and include it with the first two letters of the second word, you find *Ha'Shem karah* which means "call for HaShem [the Name]."

(3) *Isaiah 11:1–10*. The critics begin with the letter *yod* י in *Chalotzov* in 11:5 and count 72 letters backward to find *Yeshua* in 11:1. Then they begin with the *mem* מ in *Dalim* in

11:4 and count 33 letters left to right, revealing the word *Moshiach*, which ends in 11:2. Finally, they start at the letter *shin* ש in *L'mishma* in 11:3 and count 82 letters forward until they spell *sheker* at 11:7. They claim this close proximity suggests that Jesus is a false messiah.

Yacov Rambsel's position:

These critics point to the Hebrew word for "false," *sheker,* encoded at an 82-letter interval, which they identify with Yeshua the Messiah. They claim that this passage associates Jesus with the word "false" *sheker* because the name *Yeshua* is also encoded in this passage. However, if the critics would continue counting the same 82-letter intervals in reverse, beginning at the word "false" *sheker,* they would find the word "positive." When we examine Isaiah 11:1, starting with the third letter in the tenth word, counting every 82nd letter forward, we find *chashak,* which means "to cling to . . . to love . . . to desire." An entirely different meaning than the one the anti-missionary groups would suggest! Significantly, this passage, Isaiah 11:3, reveals the name *Yeshua* encoded every 88th letter forward starting from the second letter in the sixth word, which is "His eyes." When we examine this phenomenon carefully, we will find that the codes do not contradict the revelation of the Bible that Jesus is the true Messiah, the Son of God. The codes reveal that a supernatural mind must have created the Scriptures. This conclusion is confirmed countless times by the statements found in the Word of God.

In conclusion, I have studied the phenomenon of the Bible Codes for over a decade. In the last seven years, I have used computer programs to search for codes and also to verify the Bible Code discoveries made by the Israeli scientists at Hebrew University and by Yacov Rambsel. I believe that the

Bible contains a number of significant proofs that it is inspired by God. The Bible Codes are simply one additional proof that is especially meaningful to our generation in that they could not have been discovered or analyzed until the development of high-speed computers in our lifetime. I believe the primary value of the code phenomenon is to prove to this generation of skeptics that only God could inspire the human authors to record the words found in the Bible. The presence of encoded words revealing names and places of future events is a phenomenon far beyond the ability of any human author writing thousands of years ago.

NINE

A Response to Christian Critics of the Bible Codes

Several Christian writers have raised concerns about the discovery of the Bible Codes. One critic found it surprising that the Genesis study revealed the names and dates of birth or death of many prominent Jewish rabbis and sages over the last two thousand years. He asked why God would encode the names of rabbis who rejected the revelation of Jesus Christ in the New Testament. In reply, we need to understand that the presence of particular names encoded in the Bible, such as Anwar Sadat, Yitzchak Rabin, or the names of the famous rabbis, does not imply an endorsement of their lives and teachings. It simply indicates that God must be the true author of the Bible because no one else could have encoded the names of people centuries before they were born. Obviously, the discovery of the Holocaust codes, including the words *Hitler, Eichmann, Fuehrer, genocide, Holocaust, Mein Kampf, Auschwitz, Belsen,* and *king of the Nazis* within Deuteronomy and Numbers does not suggest God's approval of the evil deeds associated with the tragedy of the Holocaust. Both the Bible surface text and the embedded codes contain the names and descriptions of many people, from the most noble to the most evil.

The Yeshua codes examined in my books *The Signature of God*[1] and *The Handwriting of God*[2] glorify Jesus and reveal His divine nature as our Lord and Savior. These codes (especially the Messiah codes) reveal that it is Jesus of Nazareth who came in the flesh to fulfill the messianic prophecies. The apostle John wrote, "Hereby know ye the Spirit of God: Every spirit that confesseth that Jesus Christ is come in the flesh is of God: And every spirit that confesseth not that Jesus Christ is come in the flesh is not of God: and this is that spirit of antichrist, whereof ye have heard that it should come; and even now already is it in the world" (1 John 4:2–3). Both Rambsel and I feel that the hundreds of coded words that glorify Jesus Christ as the Messiah and Son of God are the Lord's seal of approval on the code phenomenon.

Some critics point out as well that these codes are used by the Orthodox Jewish community in seminars as evidence to convince assimilated and agnostic Jews that the Bible is authentic. The critics note that these seminars, through the use of the codes, try to convince participants that the Jewish rabbinic authorities hold a monopoly on unlocking the hidden truths of the Bible. While it is true, to some extent, that they use these codes for these purposes, it does not change the fact that the Bible Codes were created by God. No human could have created such an incredibly complex series of encoded words as we find in the Bible. In further response to the critics' suggestion that the phenomenon of the Bible Codes should be rejected simply because Orthodox rabbis use it for their own purposes, I would say that this is foolish because the same argument would demand that Christians refuse to teach from

Old Testament passages simply because the rabbis use the Hebrew Bible to teach against Christian beliefs.

Other critics have suggested that Christians should reject the Bible Codes because some Orthodox rabbis relate these codes to their teaching of the Kabbalah, Jewish mysticism, and gematria (deriving meanings from the numerical value of the Hebrew letters). Some rabbis use the Kabbalah in an attempt to find guidance, to uncover secrets, and to foretell the future. However, this argument is an example of fallacious reasoning. The fact that some people misuse the Bible Codes (like other groups misuse the Scriptures) to teach false doctrines does not provide a valid reason to reject either the Bible Codes or the Bible.

A Response to Hank Hanegraaff's "Magic Apologetics"

In an article entitled "Magic Apologetics" in the *Christian Research Institute Journal*[3] Hank Hanegraaff decries the Bible Codes phenomenon. In addition, Hanegraaff vigorously attacks me in numerous accusatory statements. Normally I do not respond to such criticism, but I feel that the issue of the validity of the Bible Codes is of sufficient importance and interest to Christian readers that I need to set the record straight. I will note, also, that Hanegraaff made no attempt to interview me about my defense of the Bible Codes. Rather, in an article flawed by false statements and errors of fact, Hanegraaff characterizes the Bible Codes as "magic apologetics" and claims that they are nothing more than "smoke and mirrors." While he is certainly entitled to his negative opinion, the false statements and gross errors in his article need to be addressed.

Hanegraaff states, "These [Bible Code] practitioners claim to have discovered such encoded prophecies as Israeli Prime Minister Yitzchak Rabin's assassination, the rise of AIDS, and detailed information regarding the Holocaust."[4] This statement is true; Hanegraaff dismisses the significance of these codes. However, the article cannot explain how twelve words about Hitler, the Holocaust, Eichmann, Nazis, Auschwitz, Poland, Berlin, Germany, Fuehrer, Mein Kampf, genocide, and crematorium could possibly appear within a few verses in Deuteronomy 10:17–22 by random chance. To date, although many have tried, no one has duplicated the phenomenon of the Bible Codes by finding thirteen key words about a future event accidentally encoded at ELS intervals in a book other than the Bible.

While it is possible to find a word such as "Somoza" at some huge ELS interval in the novel *War and Peace,* for example, no one has come close to duplicating the complex Holocaust codes or the forty-one names associated with Jesus and His disciples found in the fifteen verses of the Suffering Servant prophecy of Isaiah (Isaiah 52:13–53:12). Over the last year, Yacov Rambsel and I have challenged our critics to duplicate this experiment in any other Hebrew text. No one has found such a group of accidental ELS codes about Jesus and His disciples, despite the fact that many are trying to do so with sophisticated computer programs.

Hanegraaff continues with the following statement:

Its proponents would have us believe God has encoded secret messages in Scripture that are being discovered in these last days. Grant Jeffrey, one of its staunchest supports, calls ELS a "thrilling revelation" and "possibly the most important evidence" for the inspiration of Scripture.[5]

Here Hanegraaff suggests that I claim that there are "secret messages in Scripture." However, I have stated hundreds of times in radio and television programs, as well as in my books, that there are no secret, or hidden, messages or theological statements in the Bible Codes. In my book *The Handwriting of God* I wrote, "Bible Codes do not reveal any hidden theological sentences, teachings, or doctrines. There are no secret sentences, detailed messages, or theological statements in the encoded words. God's message of salvation and His commandments for holy living are only found in the normal, surface text of the Scriptures. The Bible Codes can only reveal key words, such as people's names, places, and occasionally, dates (using the Hebrew calendar), which provide confirmation of the supernatural inspiration and origin of the Scriptures."[6]

Hanegraaff then proposes the following example:

The following sentence will provide a clear example of the application of ELS's flawed methodology: "Paul Crouch was the cryptic treachery encoder." A computer, searching the above sentence, discovers that the twelfth letter from the right is "c." Twelve, of course, is four times three, and three is the number of the Trinity. Further computer analysis discovers the incredible "coincidence" that, taking a "trinitarian" (3 letter) leap to the left, an "r" is discovered. An esoteric code begins to emerge as the letter "i" is discovered three letters to the left of "r." Suddenly it dawns on the ELS practitioner that God may have encoded a message concerning CRI (Christian Research Institute) in the sentence above. With great anticipation, the search continues. Incredibly, ELS methodology discovers that the next word in the code is "yes." Even more amazing, we discover a quadruple trinity sequence (4 x 3 or 12) conclusion to the prophecy (i.e., nothing intelligible for the following 12 letters, a clear signal that the message is ended). What does "CRI yes" signify? The practitioner's subjective analysis inexorably leads him to the esoteric conclusion that CRI's analysis of ELS is correct. While this example might appear outrageous, it is perfectly consistent with the application of ELS in both cultic and Christian circles. In fact, the Christian application of ELS uses even more broad-ranging parameters. (footnotes omitted)[7]

Hank Hanegraaff should be embarrassed as a researcher and communicator for misleading his readers with this foolish and inaccurate example. Hanegraaff's claim that this whimsical example is "perfectly consistent with the application of ELS" cannot stand up to earnest scrutiny. Serious ELS research by Christian or Jewish researchers has nothing to do with such nonsensical rules as "Twelve, of course, is four times three, and three is the number of the Trinity." A reader who carefully examines the numerous examples of complex ELS codes provided in the original articles in *Statistical Science, Bible Review, The Signature of God, The Handwriting of God,* or Dr. Jeffrey Satinover's *Cracking the Bible Codes* will readily find that they bear not the slightest resemblance to Hanegraaff's above example in technique or in methodology.

Equally reflecting a seeming unfamiliarity with ELS code methodology is Hanegraaff's assertion: "One can search left to right, right to left, top to bottom, bottom to top, or, amazingly, even in diagonal directions. The spacing between words in the 'prophecy' can vary from word to word, and the intelligibility of the message can be just as obscure."[8] This is not how the computer searches for ELS codes at equally spaced intervals. The array or matrix that appears in research papers of some of the Israeli scientists is simply a scientific illustration of a two-dimensional array to show the compactness of the results obtained by the computer searching for ELS intervals between letters. These arrays are an illustration created after the computer has discovered an interesting ELS cluster of ELS words to demonstrate visually the "compactness" of the group of encoded words at low ELS intervals. I doubt that he has spent one hour on the computer exploring the Bible Codes reported by either the Hebrew University researchers or the Christian researchers.

Hanegraaff goes on to state, "The Christian Research Institute has denounced esoteric methods of biblical interpretation such as ELS for almost four decades. Even a cursory examination of ELS unmasks it for what it is— little more than a fringe variety of Jewish mysticism (i.e., the Cabbala) repackaged for Christian consumption. While in the past, Cabbalistic interpretations of the Torah have not been taken seriously by the Christian community, [Paul]Crouch [of Trinity Broadcasting Network] and other leaders' enthusiastic endorsements are today giving it widespread credence."[9]

Here Hanegraaff criticizes all ELS code researchers because some Jewish researchers are connected to Jewish mysticism; he puts all who study the code phenomenon into one basket, condemning every Christian ELS researcher and Jewish mystics alike. As I have stated earlier, I specifically reject any gematria or associated mystical meanings from the Kabbalah having to do with the particular ELS intervals between the Hebrew letters of encoded words. It is irrelevant whether an encoded word is spelled out at 26-letter or 37-letter intervals, for example. The relevance resides entirely in whether or not meaningful ELS words that are thematically linked can be located in a particular text of the Bible.

Hanegraaff falsely compares Bible Codes to the forbidden occult practice of numerology. But as my book *The Handwriting of God* makes clear, the ELS codes discussed by Christian researchers and writers have nothing to do with numerology, either from a spiritual or a methodological standpoint. In *The Handwriting of God,* I cautioned that God forbids any form of numerology or fortune-telling (Deuteronomy 18:9–12):

> The phenomenon of the Bible Codes has nothing to do with numerology. Numerology is defined by the author-itative Webster's Dictionary as "the study of the occult significance of numbers." Numerology is connected with divination or foretelling the future and is clearly forbidden by the Bible. There is nothing occult or secret about the codes. This phenomenon was openly pub-lished in scientific and mathematical journals, taught, and broadcast since it was first discovered thirteen years ago. The particular interval between the Hebrew letters, the actual number of letters to be skipped, has no impor-tance or significance. The codes have nothing to do with "the occult significance of numbers." Obviously, the coded words are found at various intervals (i.e., by skip-

ping 2, 7, 61, or more letters). However, the significance or meaning of the encoded word does not relate to the particular interval (the number of letters skipped). Either a particular word is spelled out in Hebrew letters at equal intervals or it is not.[10]

Hanegraaff wrongly implies a flaw in the Bible Codes phenomenon when he asserts: "It is also significant to note that none of the prophecies can be known beforehand. Jeffrey himself acknowledges that 'it is impossible to extract the encoded information unless you already know what the future facts are,' and 'the Bible prohibits us from engaging in foretelling the future.' Like Monday-morning quarterbacking, hindsight is always perfect."[11]

What Hanegraaff fails to recognize, however, is that the Bible Codes phenomenon is not flawed simply because it is impossible to find codes about a future event before the event occurs. As explained in an earlier chapter, you need to know what target words to ask the program to look for. In addition, as I have often repeated, God forbids fortune-telling.

Many of Hanegraaff's critical comments seem to be aimed at the poorly researched book by Michael Drosnin, *The Bible Codes,*[12] and its foolish predictions. Drosnin's book, however, should not be used to represent legitimate Bible Code research. Drosnin's predictions have been thoroughly refuted by every serious Jewish and Christian code researcher. Many of the code examples in Drosnin's book are inaccurate (for example, his prophecies of World War III in 1996 and a nuclear terrorist attack on Israel in 1996 have already been proven false), and many of his examples are not even valid codes. As an atheist, moreover, Drosnin doesn't care that God forbids fortune-telling.

Elaborating on his claim that legitimate Bible Codes research is "magic apologetics," Hanegraaff makes the following false statement:

> First, ELS practitioners play fast and loose with the facts. Through either carelessness or deliberate "spin doctoring," they engage in what magicians refer to as "future magic." In other words, sensationalistic embellishments are continually added as ELS stories circulate. As a case in point, the original article that stimulated interest in this arcane diversion was published without claims for any religious consequences in the journal *Statistical Science* (9:3[1994]:429–36). Subsequently a review was published in the magazine *Bible Review* (October 1985, 28–45). While virtually all of the statistical claims made for ELS are based on this article and review, Grant Jeffrey deceptively asserts that support for ELS is published "in some of the most prestigious magazines in the world," including "The British *Royal Statistical Science Journal*.". . . The only statistical journal in which the article has appeared or in which the authors discuss ELS is the *Statistical Science* article already cited. (footnotes omitted)[13]

Hanegraaff's false statement that I have deceived people plainly shows his lack of knowledge of the facts. The truth is as I have stated. The subject of ELS Codes has been published in the following prestigious magazines, including the British *Royal Statistical Science Journal* I cited:

1) D. J. Bartholomew, "Probability, Statistics and Theology," *Journal of the Royal Statistical Society,* A 151, part

1 (1988): 137–78. This article, published in 1988, contains the paper that was read before the Royal Statistical Society on Wednesday, November 11, 1987. It includes the contribution regarding ELS codes discovered by Drs. Doron Witztum, Eliyahu Rips, and Yoav Rosenberg. (See the appendix of this book for the portion of this article concerning the ELS codes.)

2) Dr. Eliyahu Rips, Dr. Yoav Rosenberg, and Dr. Doron Witztum, "Equidistant Letter Sequences in the Book of Genesis," *Statistical Science: A Review Journal of the Institute of Mathematical Statistics* 9, no. 3 (August 1994): 429–38.

3) Jeffrey Satinover, "Divine Authorship? Computer Reveals Startling Word Patterns," *Bible Review* (October 1995).

4) Jeffrey Satinover, "Responses to Divine Authorship? Computer Reveals Startling Word Patterns, and Rejoinders," *Bible Review* (February 1996).

5) Daniel Michelson, "Codes in the Torah," *B-Or Ha'Torah*, no. 6 (1987): 7–39.

6) A. M. HaSofer, "Codes in the Torah," *B-Or Ha'Torah*, no. 8E (1990): 7–39.

7) F. Eidelberg, "Codes in the Torah," *B-Or Ha'Torah*, no. 6 (1987): 7–39.

As discussed earlier in this book, other statistical studies have been completed by mathematically qualified individuals that confirm the statistical significance of several of the Yeshua and Messiah codes that Yacov Rambsel and I have found.

Hanegraaff's comment that "this [Bible Code] technique is virtually identical to those used by psychics"[14] reveals his total lack of understanding about the methods, results, and statistical calculations used by the Israeli researchers. Writing about the ELS codes and the assassination of Prime Minister Yitzchak Rabin, Hanegraaff declares,

> Using the "rigged game rules" of ELS proponents, wording extracted from the Torah, such as "Rabin, Bang, Bang," could just as easily refer to Christopher Robin's shooting his pop gun at the balloons Winnie the Pooh was holding when he floated away on the breeze in the Hundred Acre Wood! For that matter, the self-validating message could refer to the tire blow-out Batman's sidekick, Robin, experienced in the Batmobile. It could even refer to a Mafia hit man named Robino who had two successful "hits"—bang, bang. It all depends on how one validates the after-the-fact prophecies and self-validating "messages."[15]

This comment of Hanegraaff's totally ignores the multiple ELS codes discovered and documented by various codes researchers and by me in my book *The Handwriting of God*, in which I listed the following codes that obviously relate specifically to the tragic assassination of Yitzchak Rabin. For example, within the seven-verse passage of Genesis 48:13–19, we find the encoded names of *Yitzchak Rabin* and *Israel*, the day and year of Rabin's birth, the month and year of his tragic assassination, the name of his assassin *(Yigal Amir)*, the phrase *"will be murdered,"* and the word *"Oslo."*

Prime Minister Yitzchak Rabin's Assassination

Encoded Word	Hebrew	Interval	Reference Begins
Yitzchak	יצחק	(1)	Gen. 48:15
Rabin	רבין	(138)	Gen. 48:15
Will be murdered	ירצח	(85)	Gen. 48:13
Yigal	יגאל	(-241)	Gen. 48:16
Amir	עמיר	(15)	Gen. 48:15
Israel	ישראל	(1)	Gen. 48:14
5682 (Year of Rabin's birth)	התרפב	(-225)	Gen. 48:14
1st Adar (Day of Rabin's birth)	אאדר	(-177)	Gen. 48:15
5756 (Year of Rabin's death)	תשנו	(118)	Gen. 48:19
Heshvan (Month of Rabin's death)	חשון	(-285)	Gen. 48:13
Oslo	אוסלו	(182)	Gen. 49:3

Note: The year 5682 in the Hebrew calendar corresponds to 1922 in our calendar, the year Yitzchak Rabin was born. The day of his birth, the first day of Adar, occurred on our March 1. The month Heshvan in the Hebrew calendar year 5756 corresponds to November 1995, when the assassination occurred.

Hanegraaff claims that "Muslims have used both numerics and ELS in a vain attempt to prove that Allah is the only true God and Muhammad is his prophet. In addition, they use these methods to 'prove' that Christianity is false."[16] My own research would not support Hanegraaff's claim; after years of research and examination of Muslim

Internet sites, I am unaware of any claims by Muslims that they have found ELS codes in the Koran. While a few Muslims have falsely claimed the existence of a very simple pattern of the number 19 found in their religious book, every serious statistical examination of this claim has proven it is false. In addition, virtually all Muslim scholars have rejected this unsupported claim. However, this Muslim claim regarding a pattern of 19 in the Koran has nothing to do with Bible Codes. An article that disproves these false claims about the number 19 can be viewed at the following Web site: http://www.math.gatech.edu/~jkatz/Religions/Numerics/.

In discussing the Jewish group Aish Ha Torah (Hebrew for "Man of the Law"), which promotes worldwide ELS Discovery Seminars, Hanegraaff writes, "They also use ELS to 'prove' that Jesus Christ was a false Messiah." However, as demonstrated in chapter 8, the chapter discussing Israeli critics of the Bible Codes, Aish Ha Torah's claims are false.

It appears that Hanegraaff is relying upon a critical attack on the Yeshua codes by Rabbi Daniel Mechanic that appeared on the Internet and that Hanegraaff is unaware of the detailed rebuttal to that attack. The article by Rabbi Mechanic, a major spokesman for the Jewish Aish Ha Torah group, is entitled "Jesus Codes: Uses and Abuses." It vigorously attacks the discovery of the Yeshua codes published by Yacov Rambsel and me. However, that article was thoroughly refuted in an Internet article by Guy Cramer and Lori Eldridge entitled "Statistical Significance Discovered in the Yeshua Codes." The article's statistical study (which remains undisputed after a year on the Internet) disproves Rabbi Mechanic's theory that none of the Yeshua codes found by Yacov Rambsel has any statistical significance. Several mathematicians have analyzed the statistical study of the Yeshua codes, including one who replied, "I have no problem with your calculations of significance for these phrases." To date, no mathematician has challenged the calculations that appear in the earlier chapter. This article can be found at the following URL address on the Internet: http://www.prophezine.com/tcode/index.shtml.

Hanegraaff concludes his assessment of the Bible Code phenomenon with the comment that, "Finally, ELS shifts the focus of biblical apologetics from the essential core of the Gospel—the death, burial, and resurrection of Christ (1 Cor. 15:1–4)—to esoteric speculations. . . . Every form of apologetics must begin and eventually return to the resurrection of Jesus Christ as the most well attested fact of ancient history. Despite the claims of men like Paul Crouch and Grant Jeffrey, those who deny the incontrovertible evidence for the Resurrection are not likely to embrace the magic and misleading apologetic of ELS."[17]

This criticism of my approach to the Bible Codes is entirely misplaced. As my books that discuss the codes make abundantly clear, these codes were introduced as only one among a number of standard apologetic proofs for the reliability of the Word of God, including archeology, advanced scientific and medical statements in the Bible, and fulfilled prophecies, which *together* support the absolute credibility of the inspiration and authority of the Scriptures. The whole purpose of my ministry and books is to direct men and women to the claims of Jesus Christ as our Savior and Lord. Each one of my eight books contains a final chapter that invites the reader to accept Christ based upon the historically proven facts of the "death, burial, and resurrection of Christ."

Unfortunately, many of the Christian critics of the Bible Code phenomenon have simply repeated the criticisms of the Orthodox Jewish critics or the atheists, who reject the authority of the Bible altogether. Rather than completing their own detailed research, which should involve discussions with Christian authors who have written about the Bible Codes, these critics have been content to repeat the criticisms of those who reject the inspiration of the Bible and those who reject Jesus as the Messiah.

Why would God have placed Bible Codes in the Scriptures that would not be discovered until the final generation of this millennium? Only He knows. However, I would suggest that God knew that our generation would be filled with skepticism and doubt more than any other generation in history. The Bible has suffered relentless attacks in the last eighty years, which has caused many pastors and laymen to abandon their confidence in the authority and inspiration of the Scriptures. If these codes are genuine, and I believe they are, they were placed there by God to speak to those in this generation who deny the supernatural inspiration of the Scriptures.

My argument is simply this: No human could have produced these incredibly complex codes. In addition, the codes glorify and lift up the name of Jesus Christ. Therefore, I conclude that they may prove useful in witnessing to the inspiration of the Bible and stand alongside the other standard apologetic evidence, such as the archeological and historical evidence, the advanced scientific and medical knowledge in the Bible, and the evidence from fulfilled prophecy. If we use this material wisely and carefully, in conjunction with the other evidence, we can fulfill God's command to us in 1 Peter 3:15: "But sanctify the Lord God in your hearts: and be ready always to give an answer to every man that asketh you a reason of the hope that is in you with meekness and fear."

TEN

The Discovery of Bible Codes in the Greek New Testament

I have known about the existence of Bible Codes in the Hebrew Old Testament for over a decade. During that time, I often wondered whether it might be possible to discover similar ELS patterns in the Greek New Testament. Many Christians who know about the Bible Codes have wondered why God would place complex ELS patterns in the Hebrew Old Testament and not place them in the Greek New Testament as well. While I heard vague reports from time to time that such patterns had been found in the New Testament, I could never get confirmation of these reports. During the last few months, however, I began to work with several computer programmers on a fascinating project to test the theory that meaningful ELS words exist within the Greek New Testament. The programmers acquired a computer program that contained the complete Greek New Testament text from the German Bible Society. This biblical text is known as the textus receptus (received text), which is the same Greek text used by the King James translators in 1611. This text is also used by the Wycliffe Bible Translators worldwide as the basis for their translation of the Greek

New Testament into foreign languages. The programmers created a software program that would search through the entire Bible from Genesis to Revelation to find meaningful target words at equal skip intervals in both the Hebrew and Greek texts.

During a week of initial research with the new program, developed by BibleFind Research Center, I found some fascinating ELS patterns that I will share in this chapter. Obviously, the research on the Greek text is just beginning, but the initial discoveries suggest that we will ultimately discover that the Greek New Testament contains the same complex pattern of Bible Codes that has been verified in the Old Testament.

The Jesus Codes

There are 7,914 verses in the New Testament that cover a remarkable number of subjects. To focus this study, I searched first for those verses in which the name *Jesus* appears encoded with the smallest ELS skip distance. The name *Jesus* in Greek is spelled *Ιησου*. When I searched the whole of the New Testament with the computer for the word *Jesus Ιησου* at minimum skip intervals of 22 letters or less, I found nineteen verses in which the name *Jesus* is encoded. Significantly, although there are almost eight thousand verses in the New Testament, most of these nineteen ELS codes spelling the name *Jesus* are found in very important verses that clearly deal with teachings about Jesus or key statements by Christ Himself. Furthermore, other key words associated with Jesus, such as Lamb and Nazareth, are found encoded in the same passage.

Jesus Iησου, "The Name of the Son of God" (1 John 5:13)

In my research, I discovered that the absolute minimum skip interval (5-letter intervals) for the name *Jesus Iησου* in the whole of the New Testament is found in 1 John 5:13: "These things have I written unto you that believe on the name of the Son of God; that ye may know that ye have eternal life, and that ye may believe on the name of the Son of God." Note that this Bible Code, *Jesus,* is found in one of the most significant verses in the New Testament, a verse that declares that our hope for eternal life depends on our believing on the name of the Son of God. The verse that draws our attention to the significance of believing on the name of the Son of God actually contains the name of God's Son, *Jesus Iησου,* encoded at 5-letter skip intervals!

Ταυτα εγραψα υμιν τοις πιστευουσιν εις το ονομα του υιου του θεου ινα ειδητε οτι ζωην εχετε αιωνιον και ινα πιστευητε εις το ονομα του υιου του θεου. (1 John 5:13)

These things have I written unto you that believe on the name of the Son of God; that ye may know that ye have eternal life, and that ye may believe on the name of the Son of God. (1 John 5:13)

This discovery might cause an inquiring mind to ask the following question: Does this occurrence of *Jesus Iησου* encoded at 5-letter intervals actually refer to Jesus of Nazareth? In an attempt to answer this question, I examined the text closely to see if any other meaningful ELS words could be located that might help us determine if this Bible

Code actually refers to Jesus Christ. Intriguingly, the word *Nazareth Νασαρα*, the city where Jesus grew up and the source of the name *Jesus of Nazareth,* is also encoded in this paragraph, beginning in 1 John 5:5 and skipping forward at an interval of 73 letters. The word *Nazareth* was found to be encoded only eighteen times in the New Testament. However, *Nazareth* is encoded only one time at an ELS interval of less than 100 letters in the seven New Testament books beginning with the epistle of James through the book of Jude (417 verses). In other words, this encoded word *Nazareth* occurs vary rarely. Therefore, the appearance of the word *Nazareth* in this powerful passage provides strong evidence that this is a genuine Bible Code identifying Jesus of Nazareth that was purposely placed in this epistle of John. Another encoded word in the same verse is "lamb," reminding us of Jesus' title as the *Lamb of God*. The word *Lamb Αμνοσ* is encoded in 1 John 5:13 at 2-letter intervals, in the same verse in which *Jesus Ιησου* is encoded at 5-letter intervals.

Words Associated with Jesus Encoded in 1 John 5:13

Encoded Word	Greek	Interval	Reference Begins
Jesus	*Ιησου*	(5)	1 John 5:13
Nazareth	*Νασαρα*	(73)	1 John 5:5
Lamb	*Αμνοσ*	(54)	1 John 5:13

Jesus *Ιησου* Encoded in Matthew 24:30

Jesus' prophecy in Matthew 24:30 concludes His revelation

of the series of prophetic events that will culminate in His glorious return from heaven to usher in the Millennial Kingdom of God on earth. The second smallest minimum skip interval in the New Testament for the name *Jesus Ιησου* is found in Matthew 24:30, in which it is encoded every 8th letter. This verse announces the majestic return of Jesus Christ as the King of Kings:

> And then shall appear the sign of the Son of man in heaven: and then shall all the tribes of the earth mourn, and they shall see the Son of man coming in the clouds of heaven with power and great glory. (Matthew 24:30)

It is fascinating to discover that the following words associated with Jesus of Nazareth are also encoded in Christ's great prophecy of Matthew 24.

Words Associated with Jesus Encoded in Matthew 24:30

Encoded Word	Greek	Interval	Reference Begins
Jesus	Ιησου	(8)	Matt. 24:30
Nazareth	Νασαρα	(84)	Matt. 24:36
Mercy	Ελεοσ	(62)	Matt. 24:48
Lamb	Αμνοσ	(50)	Matt. 24:7

Jesus Ιησου Encoded in Mark 8:35

In Mark 8:35, Jesus taught that the true value in a Christian's life is demonstrated by His disciple's willingness to "lose his life for my sake" so that "the same shall save it." The name *Jesus Iησου* is found encoded in this passage at a minimal skip interval of every sixteen letters. In the verse that precedes this passage, Jesus commanded that, "Whosoever will come after me, let him deny himself, and take up his cross, and follow me" (Mark 8:34). Significantly, I found a series of Bible Codes that relate specifically to Jesus in this same passage:

> For whosoever will save his life shall lose it; but whoso-ever shall lose his life for my sake and the gospel's, the same shall save it. (Mark 8:35)

The words blood, innocent, and lamb encoded in this passage remind us of Christ's supreme sacrifice on the cross for our salvation. Also, the appearance of the name Jonah encoded in this same verse may suggest an analogy between Jonah's willingness to sacrifice his life by offering to be thrown into the sea to save those on board the ship and Jesus' willingness to offer His life as a sacrifice for the sins of all those who would repent and turn from their wicked rebellion against God.

Words Associated with *Jesus Iησου*
Encoded in Mark 8:35

Encoded Word	Greek	Interval	Reference Begins
Jesus	*Iησου*	(16)	Mark 8:35
Blood	*Aιμα*	(52)	Mark 8:8
Son	*υιοσ*	(3)	Mark 8:25
Innocent	*Aθωοσ*	(2)	Mark 8:24
Lamb	*Aμνοσ*	(3)	Mark 9:2

Jonah   *Ιωνασ*   (97)   Mark 8:3

Jesus Ιησου Encoded at Very Low ELS Intervals

A number of other Bible Codes revealing the name *Jesus Ιησου* were located at very low skip intervals in the New Testament. Consider the spiritual importance of these passages in light of the very small probability that these particular encoded words would appear in these specific verses by random chance. The following list contains the most significant of these verses in which *Jesus Ιησου* occurs at intervals of 22 letters or less. Note that these key verses relate directly to the life, ministry, and second coming of Jesus Christ.

List of Verses with *Jesus Ιησου* at Very Low ELS intervals

Matthew 14:23: "And when he had sent the multitudes away, he went up into a mountain apart to pray: and when the evening was come, he was there alone." The name *Jesus Ιησου* is encoded every 13th letter in this passage that describes Jesus walking on the Sea of Galilee.

Matthew 16:24: "Then said Jesus unto his disciples, If any man will come after me, let him deny himself, and take up his cross, and follow me." In this key passage in which Christ calls us to become disciples, the name *Jesus Ιησου* is encoded every 16th letter.

Mark 13:32: "But of that day and that hour knoweth no man, no, not the angels which are in heaven, neither the Son, but the Father." Here in this important verse regarding the timing of Christ's second coming, the name *Jesus Ιησου* is encoded every 17th letter.

Luke 9:24: "For whosoever will save his life shall lose it: but whosoever will lose his life for my sake, the same shall save it." Note that the name *Jesus Ιησου* is encoded every 16th letter in this passage, which is a parallel passage to Mark 8:35.

John 4:6: "Now Jacob's well was there. Jesus therefore, being wearied with his journey, sat thus on the well: and it was about the sixth hour." The name *Jesus Ιησου* is encoded every 18th letter in this verse in which Jesus begins to witness to the woman at the well about salvation through His "living water."

John 21:17: "He saith unto him the third time, Simon, son of Jonas, lovest thou me? Peter was grieved because he said unto him the third time, Lovest thou me? And he said unto him, Lord, thou knowest all things; thou knowest that I love thee. Jesus saith unto him, Feed my sheep." In this verse in which Christ commands each of us to spiritually minister to other Christians, we find the name *Jesus Ιησου* encoded every 7th letter. That is the second smallest minimal skip interval for *Jesus* in the New Testament.

Romans 8:34: "Who is he that condemneth? It is Christ that died, yea rather, that is risen again, who is even at the right hand of God, who also maketh intercession for us." The apostle Paul's teaching about Christ's resurrection contains the name *Jesus Ιησου*, encoded every 22nd letter.

Galatians 3:27: "For as many of you as have been baptized into Christ have put on Christ." This important passage about baptism contains the name *Jesus Ιησου*, encoded every 17th letter. However, the computer search revealed the word *Jonah*, encoded every 12th letter just before this passage, while the word *Son* is encoded in Galatians 3:26 every 3 letters.

Colossians 3:11: "Where there is neither Greek nor Jew, circumcision nor uncircumcision, Barbarian, Scythian, bond nor free: but Christ is all, and in all." While the name *Jesus* *Ιησου* is encoded every 10th letter in this verse, it is interesting to note that the word *Innocent* is also encoded every 2nd letter beginning in Colossians 3:9.

1 John 3:17: "But whoso hath this world's good, and seeth his brother have need, and shutteth up his bowels of compassion from him, how dwelleth the love of God in him?" The name *Jesus* *Ιησου* is encoded every 13th letter. However, the word *love* is also encoded every 18 letters in the same passage that commands us to demonstrate our love of others.

Jude 4: "For there are certain men crept in unawares, who were before of old ordained to this condemnation, ungodly men, turning the grace of our God into lasciviousness, and denying the only Lord God, and our Lord Jesus Christ." This key verse, warning of the coming apostasy when some will deny Jesus Christ as our Lord, contains the name *Jesus* *Ιησου*, encoded every 20th letter.

The Name *Jesus* *Ιησου* Encoded in Matthew 27:9

Matthew records the fulfillment of the prophecy that the exact price of the Messiah's betrayal would be "thirty pieces of silver." I discovered that this important verse regarding the fulfillment of messianic prophecies in Christ's life contains the name *Jesus* *Ιησου*, encoded every 41 letters:

Then was fulfilled that which was spoken by Jeremy the
prophet, saying, And they took the thirty pieces of silver,

the price of him that was valued, whom they of the children of Israel did value. (Matthew 27:9)

However, it is intriguing to find that this passage also contains a series of important Bible Codes that relate to Jesus of Nazareth: *lamb, blood, savior,* and *Nazareth.*

Jesus *Ιησου* Encoded in Matthew 27:9

Encoded Word	Greek	Interval	Reference Begins
Nazareth	*Νασαρα*	(84)	Matt. 27:22
Jesus	*Ιησου*	(41)	Matt. 17:22
Blood	*Αιμα*	(44)	Matt. 27:32
Savior	*Αθωοσ*	(10)	Matt. 27:45
Lamb	*Αμνοσ*	(93)	Matt. 27:51

In this initial study I have discovered a number of meaningful ELS encoded words connected with Jesus of Nazareth that appear in key passages of the Greek New Testament. While this initial study is extremely limited because the researchers have just developed the computer program to examine the Greek text, the initial results suggest that ultimately we may find that the Bible Codes in the New Testament are just as complex and significant as they are in the Old Testament.

Obviously, much work remains to be done. My research team has decided to make our computer program available on the Internet to allow any interested researcher to personally examine the Greek text for Bible Codes. This unique computer search program is designed to search for ELS patterns in both the Hebrew text of the Old Testament, as well as the Greek text of the New Testament. This Internet Web site will include all verified discoveries made by researchers to date, in both the Hebrew and the Greek Scriptures. For the first time, those who are fascinated by the Bible Codes will be able to use this software search engine to personally search for Bible Codes through the whole Bible, from Genesis to Revelation. After verification, genuine ELS code discoveries made by visitors to this Web site will be published on a page on our Web site for examination by other interested readers. By this means, we hope to build up a permanent library of recognized, verified, and significant Bible Codes that have been discovered by both Jewish and Christian researchers.

In addition, we hope to interest mathematicians and statisticians to examine several of the Hebrew and Greek Bible Codes to determine whether or not they can be statistically proven to be beyond the probability of random chance. By making our search engine, BibleFind Research Center, available to any interested researcher, we hope to expand interest in this phenomenon. The new program developed by our team is now available on the Internet to allow you to search for fascinating ELS patterns and to explore the discoveries of other students of the Bible. The URL address of the BibleFind Research Center Web site is http://www.BibleFind.com. My own Web site featuring both Bible Code discoveries and my continuing research on other topics is http://www.grantjeffrey.com.

ELEVEN

The Implications of the Bible Codes

While individuals can challenge the significance of particular ELS word patterns, the discovery of dozens of Bible Codes revealing details about historical events that occurred thousands of years after the Bible was written is a unique validation in our lifetime of the inspiration and authority of the Scriptures as the Word of God. Although the Bible Codes are fascinating, it is important to place them in their proper context. In my earlier books, *The Signature of God* and *The Handwriting of God,* I explored the fields of history, archeology, and fulfilled prophecy, as well as advanced scientific and medical statements in the Bible that together provide powerful evidence that the Scriptures are God's genuine revelation to humanity. Ultimately, the true significance of the Bible Codes is that they communicate the message of the Bible's inspiration to our skeptical generation in a unique and scientific manner.

The Bible itself continually affirms that it is inspired by God. The apostle Paul wrote, "All scripture is given by inspiration of God, and is profitable for doctrine, for reproof, for correction, for instruction in righteousness" (2 Timothy

3:16). In light of the evidence that the Bible does provide us with a genuine revelation of the purposes of God, it is important that we consider these words of Jesus Christ: "Whom say you that I am?" Jesus posed this question to His disciples during a conversation that took place in the region of Caesarea Philippi: "He asked his disciples, saying, Whom do men say that I the Son of man am? And they said, Some say that thou art John the Baptist: some, Elias; and others, Jeremias, or one of the prophets. He saith unto them, But whom say ye that I am? And Simon Peter answered and said, Thou art the Christ, the Son of the living God" (Matthew 16:13–16).

Jesus Christ's question—"Whom say you that I am?"—is one of the most fundamental and important questions we will ever answer. Our answer to His question will determine our present happiness, the forgiveness of our sins, and our eternal reconciliation with God in heaven. If we reject the claims of Jesus as the true Son of God, we choose, in effect, to be our own gods—living as if we are the supreme beings in our lives. The eternal consequences of such a choice are beyond the scope of human language to adequately express. If we reject the only salvation that God offers us through Jesus Christ, we will end our lives as unrepentant sinners in permanent rebellion against God.

Throughout the Scriptures, we read the claim that Jesus is the Messiah, the Son of God. Furthermore, the Bible declares that His death on the cross is the only acceptable sacrifice that can pay the full price of our sins. The apostle Paul warns of the eternal consequences of our rebellion in his epistle to the Christians at Rome: "For the wages of sin is death; but the gift of God is eternal life through Jesus Christ our Lord" (Romans 6:23). As a result of our sins, each of us has walked away from God in disobedience. The problem faced by every human is this: How can we be reconciled to a Holy God when we have rebelled against Him all our lives? Every person who has lived on earth has rebelled against God and lived life as a sinner. The apostle Paul declared, "For all have sinned, and come short of the glory of God" (Romans 3:23).

There is nothing in our sinful nature that enables us to totally reform and stop sinning. Even if the impossible occurred and we never sinned from this moment on, we would still be barred from the holiness of heaven because of our past sins. The only way to live with God in heaven after this sinful life is to become holy and righteous. However, it is obviously impossible for us to accomplish this on our own. Paul declares that the only way we will "see the Lord" is by walking in "holiness": "Follow peace with all men, and holiness, without which no man shall see the Lord" (Hebrews 12:14). But how can a person become holy before God?

The Lord knew that spiritually transforming those of us willing to repent of our sins was the only way we could ever be reconciled to Him and become fit to enter heaven. Paul explained God's purpose in offering salvation to anyone who would confess their sins: "To the end he may stablish your hearts unblameable in holiness before God, even our Father, at the coming of our Lord Jesus Christ with all his saints" (1 Thessalonians 3:13).

The most important decision you will ever make is what you will do with the written revelation of God found in the Bible. Your decision as to whether or not the Bible is truly the inspired Word of God will profoundly affect every other area of your life. If the Bible is true, then you and I are accountable to Jesus Christ, and He will judge each one of us at the end of our life. However, if the Bible is not the inspired Word of God, we can ignore its commands and warnings about heaven and hell. In the absence of the written revelation found in the Word of God, those of us who search for ultimate truth are lost and without any hope of finding it.

In light of the overwhelming evidence presented in *The Mysterious Bible Codes* regarding the inspiration and authority of the Bible, any unbiased person can conclude that only God could have inspired the writers of the Bible. The evidence in this book proves that the Scriptures contain Bible Codes about historical events that only God could have known. However, there are many people in our generation who cannot accept the claims of the Bible. The problem with many readers who still refuse to acknowledge the evidence that the Bible is the inspired Word of God is not one of conviction; rather, it is their lack of willingness to accept information that challenges their long-held positions. It is extremely difficult for most people to abandon the agnostic positions they have defended for years and admit that they were wrong. Those who have previously rejected God and the Bible have a huge emotional and intellectual investment in their declared position of agnosticism or rejection of the Scriptures. Many people refuse to submit to the truth of the Word of God because they fear the changes in daily life, habits, and priorities that the Word of God will force them to make.

When faced with the powerful Bible Codes evidence that the Bible is truly inspired by God, these people naturally feel threatened because they must now think seriously about God and their responsibility to Him. Many people have never seriously considered the claims of the Gospels about Jesus Christ. Their previous casual denial of the authority of the Bible has shielded them against asking tough questions such as: What if the Bible is true? What if there truly is a heaven, a hell, and the possibility of eternal separation from God? Where will I spend eternity? How can I be assured that I will go to heaven?

In light of the evidence presented in this book, we need to carefully consider the implications of this proof that the Bible is God's genuine revelation. If the Bible is truly the Word of God, then each one of us will someday stand before Jesus Christ at the end of our life to answer His question: "Who do you say that I am?" (Matthew 16:15 NASB). On that day, those who have accepted Christ's offer of salvation through His sacrifice on the cross will greet Jesus with great joy, knowing that God has forgiven their sins. Their destiny will be to live in joy and peace with Christ forever in heaven. However, those who have chosen in the end to reject the Bible and Christ's offer of salvation will be forced by their decision to bear the punishment for their sins in hell forever.

Many in our modern religiously pluralistic society are offended by the fact that the Bible declares that there is only one possible way to be saved. However, the apostle Paul spoke about the absolute necessity of faith in Jesus Christ: "Neither is there salvation in any other: for there is none other name under heaven given among men, whereby we must be saved" (Acts 4:12). Paul's declaration runs counter to the natural inclination of mankind to believe that all religions are equally true and that "all roads lead to Rome."

Many people would like to believe that, as long as they are sincere and live a reasonably decent and good life, they will make it to heaven. This is a lie from the pit of hell. The Word of God declares that sincerity is not enough. If you are sincere in your faith but choose to reject Jesus Christ and to place your faith in a false religion, then you are sincerely wrong and lost for eternity. Why would Jesus Christ have willingly died on the cross for your sins if there were other equally valid ways for you to be reconciled to God?

Some people suggest that if God is truly a God of love, then somehow He will be "kind" and bend the rules to allow "good" people into heaven, despite their lifelong rejection of Jesus Christ's gift of salvation. Consider the implications of this proposition for a moment. If the Lord allowed unrepentant sinners who reject Christ into heaven, He would have to deny His nature as a holy and just God. Admitting unrepentant sinners into heaven would, in effect, transform heaven into an annex of hell. If unrepentant souls were allowed into heaven, their sin would pollute the holiness of heaven. The sinless nature of a holy heaven and the evil nature of sin make it impossible for God to forgive men's sins unless they wholeheartedly repent and turn from sin. God can forgive and transform by His Spirit only those who repent and are saved by the grace of Jesus Christ, who cleanses us from our sins. Although we can cleanse our bodies with water, the cleansing of our souls requires the spiritual application of the blood of Christ to our hearts.

The sole entrance requirement into heaven is your relationship to Jesus Christ. God demands perfect holiness and righteousness. However, it is obvious that we cannot meet these requirements on our own merit. Since God can never ignore the fact that we have sinned against Him, it was necessary that someone who was perfect and sinless should pay the penalty of physical and spiritual death as a substitute for us. The only person who could qualify was Jesus Christ, the Holy Son of God.

Christ's sacrificial gift of His life on the cross paid the price for our sins. Every one of us, by accepting His pardon, can stand before the judgment seat of God clothed in Christ's righteousness: "For he hath made him [Jesus] to be sin for us, who knew no sin; that we might be made the righteousness of God in him" (2 Corinthians 5:21). Christ's atonement is, perhaps, the greatest mystery in creation. Jesus is the only one in history who, by His sinless life, was qualified to enter heaven. Yet, He loved each one of us so much that He chose to die upon that cross to purchase our salvation. In a marvelous act of God's mercy, the righteousness of Jesus is placed to our account with God.

When Nicodemus, one of the righteous religious leaders of Israel, came to Jesus, he asked Him about salvation. Jesus responded, "Verily, verily, I say unto thee, Except a man be born again, he cannot see the kingdom of God" (John 3:3). It isn't simply a matter of intellectually accepting the facts about Christ and salvation. To be "born again" you must sincerely repent of your sinful life, ask God to forgive you, and wholeheartedly place your trust in Jesus Christ. This decision will transform your destiny forever. God will give you a new purpose and meaning. The Lord promises believers eternal life in heaven: "This is the will of him that sent me, that everyone who seeth the Son, and believeth in him, may have everlasting life; and I will raise him up at the last day" (John 6:40). The moment you commit your life to Christ, you will receive eternal life. Though your body will someday die, you will live forever with Christ in heaven. Jesus explained to Nicodemus, "For God so loved the world, that he gave his only begotten Son, that whosoever believeth in him should not perish, but have everlasting life" (John 3:16).

Your decision to accept Jesus Christ as your personal Savior is the most important decision you will ever make. This commitment will lift the guilt of sin from your heart and give you an abundant new life in Jesus. And there is more; the Lord Jesus Christ asks His disciples to "follow Me." Your commitment to Christ will transform your life into one of joy, peace, and spiritual purpose beyond anything you have ever known. Jesus challenges each of us to consider the choices of life in terms of eternity, "For what shall it profit a man, if he shall gain the whole world, and lose his own soul?" (Mark 8:36).

If you are already a follower of Jesus Christ, I encourage you to discuss this book with your friends and family as an effective way to share your faith in Christ. The evidence that the Bible is inspired by a supernatural God will not, of itself, lead anyone to a personal faith in Christ. That decision to follow Christ is a fundamental choice to choose spiritual life over spiritual death by responding to Christ's offer of salvation. However, it is my prayer that the evidence of the Bible Codes presented in this book may help someone to seriously consider the claims of Jesus Christ for the first time.

The Statistics

I am quoting from the original 1988 article by Drs. Witztum, Rips, and Rosenberg dealing with the ELS codes in Genesis that led to the controversy about whether or not such an article existed. The editor of the *Journal of the Royal Statistical Society* provided me with a photocopy of the original article when I visited their offices in London. The following quotations provide readers with the relevant portion of the original paper that dealt with the phenomenon of the ELS codes in Genesis.

Journal of the Royal Statistical Society, A151, part 1 (1988): 137–78, "Probability, Statistics and Theology"

By D. J. Bartholomew (Read before the Royal Statistical Society on Wednesday, November 11, 1987):

The broad class of questions facing us concerns whether it is reasonable, on the evidence of nature and history, to infer that the universe had its origin in the action of a supreme being and, if so, what can be learnt about the purposes and nature of that being. [The following portion of the paper was written by the Israeli ELS researchers Doron Witztum (Jerusalem College of Technology),

Eliyahu Rips (The Hebrew University of Jerusalem) and
Yoav Rosenberg (Jerusalem College of Technology):]

Our main progress is the discovery of a systematic
quantifiable pattern, which allows us to apply usual statistical methods for the estimation of its significance. We
consider the Book of Genesis as a string of letters, all
spaces being excluded—denote this string G. An
equidistant letter sequence (ELS) is defined as the
sequence of letters in G found at positions

$$n, n + d, n + 2d, ..., n + (k—I)d.$$

I have omitted the balance of the statistical calculations contained in this 1988 article. The Israeli researchers
concluded their portion of this paper with the following
comment:

No control tests showed significant deviation from a
uniform distribution. For the string G, however for the
unperturbed sample (which contains more than 300
word pairs), we obtained $c(w, w')$ tending to zero with a
probability against the null hypothesis of a uniform distribution that we estimate as $1.8 \times 10–17$.

List of Hebrew Words for Researchers

Many readers have expressed interest in searching for Bible
Codes with the variety of computer programs that are
available commercially or those which can be accessed on
the Internet. As I mentioned in chapter 10, the BibleFind
Research Center team of computer programmers who
developed the search engine to explore both the Hebrew

text of the Old Testament and the Greek text of the New Testament can be accessed at the following Web site: http://www.BibleFind.com. I strongly recommend the interested reader also acquire an excellent Hebrew - English Dictionary and a Hebrew-Greek-English Interlinear Bible from your Christian bookstore.

Notes

Introduction

1. Glueck, Nelson, *Rivers in the Desert: History of the Negev* (Philadelphia: Jewish Publications Society of America, 1969).

2. Butler, Joseph, *The Analogy of Religion* (London: H. Morley Co., 1884).

3. Michelson, D., "Codes in the Torah." *B'Or Ha'Torah*, no. 6 (1987): 31.

4. Ibid.

5. Jeffrey, Grant R, *The Signature of God* (Toronto: Frontier Research Publications, 1996).

Chapter 1

1. S. Davidson, *Introduction to the Old Testament* (1856) 89.

Chapter 2

1. Rabbi Moses Cordevaro.

2. Louis Ginzberg, *The Legends of the Jews* (Philadelphia: The Jewish Publication Society of America, 1968).

3. Jeffrey Satinover, *Cracking the Bible Codes* (New York: William Morrow and Co. Inc., 1997) 314.

4. Ibid.

Chapter 3

1. D.J. Bartholomew, "Probability, Statistics, and Theology," *Journal of the Royal Statistical Society* A151, Part 1 (1988): 137-38.

2. Jeffrey Satinover, "Divine Inspiration?," *Bible Review* Nov. 1995.

3. D.J. Bartholomew, "Probability, Statistics, and Theology," *Journal of the Royal Statistical Society* A151, Part 1 (1988): 137-138.

4. M. Margalioth, ed., *Encyclopedia of Great Men in Israel,* 1961.

5. Robert Kass, "Equidistant Letter Sequences in the Book of Genesis," *Statistical Science* Aug. 1994.

6. Jeffrey Satinover, *Bible Review* Feb. 1996.

7. Doron Witztum and Maymad HaNosaf, *The Added Dimension* (Jerusalem: Agudah L/Machkor Torani, 1989).

Chapter 4

1. Michael Drosnin, *The Bible Code* (New York: Simon and Schuster, 1997).

Chapter 5

1. Senator Jesse Helms, letter, March. 1996.

2. Moshe Katz, *Computorah* (Jerusalem: Achdut Printing, 1996).

3. Grant Jeffrey, *The Signature of God* (Toronto: Frontier Research Publications, 1996).

Chapter 6

1. Yacov Rambsel, *YESHUA: The Name of Jesus Revealed in the Old Testament* (Toronto: Frontier Research Publications, 1996).

2. Ibid.

3. Guy Cramer and Lori Eldridge, "Statistical Significance Discovered in the Yeshua Codes," Internet, 1997.

4. Rabbi Moses Maimonides, *Mishneh Torah,* ed. Rabbi Eliyahu Touger (New York: Maznaim, 1987).

5. Rabbi Maimonides, *The Laws of Kings and Their Wars* (New York: Maznaim, 1987) 234-35.

Chapter 8

1. Grant Jeffrey, *The Signature of God* (Toronto: Frontier Research Publications, 1996).

Chapter 9

1. Grant Jeffrey, *The Signature of God* (Toronto: Frontier Research Publications, 1996).

2. Grant Jeffrey, *The Handwriting of God* (Toronto: Frontier Research Publications, 1996).

3. Hank Hanegraaff, "Magic Apologetics," *Christian Research Institute Journal* Sept./Oct. 1997.

4. Ibid.

5. Ibid.

6. Grant Jeffrey, *The Handwriting of God* (Toronto: Frontier Research Publications, 1996).

7. Hank Hanegraaff, "Magic Apologetics," *Christian Research Institute Journal* Sept./Oct. 1997.

8. Ibid.

9. Ibid.

10. Grant Jeffrey, *The Handwriting of God* (Toronto: Frontier Research Publications, 1996).

11. Hank Hanegraaff, "Magic Apologetics," *Christian Research Institute Journal* Sept./Oct. 1997.

12. Michael Drosnin, *The Bible Code* (New York: Simon and Schuster, 1997).

13. Hank Hanegraaff, "Magic Apologetics," *Christian Research Institute Journal* Sept./Oct. 1997.

14. Ibid.

15. Ibid.

16. Ibid.

17. Ibid.